A DAY IN THE LIFE
OF A POO, A GNU AND YOU

EDITED BY JONNY LEIGHTON
DESIGNED BY JACK CLUCAS
COVER DESIGN BY ANGIE ALLISON
SPECIAL THANKS TO LAUREN FARNSWORTH

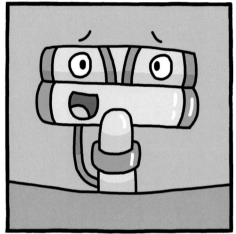

First published in Great Britain in 2020 by Buster Books,
an imprint of Michael O'Mara Books Limited, 9 Lion Yard,
Tremadoc Road, London SW4 7NQ

W www.mombooks.com/buster   f Buster Books   🐦 @BusterBooks   📷 @Buster_Books

Text and layout © Mike Barfield 2020

Illustrations copyright © Buster Books 2020

A CIP catalogue record for this book is available from the British Library.

ISBN: 978-1-78055-646-8

3 5 7 9 10 8 6 4 2

This book was printed in January 2021 by Shenzhen Wing King
Tong Paper Products Co. Ltd., Shenzhen, Guangdong, China.

A DAY IN THE LIFE
OF A POO, A GNU AND YOU

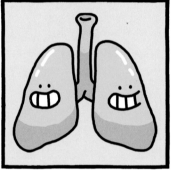

WRITTEN BY **MIKE BARFIELD**
ILLUSTRATED BY **JESS BRADLEY**

Buster Books

CONTENTS

INTRODUCTION

Welcome to *A Day in the Life of a Poo, a Gnu and You*, a laugh-out-loud guide to life on Earth (and in some cases, beyond).

This book is split into three sections: Human Body, Animal Kingdom and Earth and Science. If you've ever wanted to know what's going on inside your body, what animals get up to when you're not watching or the science behind how things in our world work, then look no further.

There are **Day in the Life** comics that give you a snapshot of just what things get up to all day, **Bigger Picture** pages that provide extra info and handy diagrams, plus **Secret Diaries** that will let you into all sorts of inside knowledge.

You'll also find a Glossary at the back of the book, which will help explain any tricky words you come across along the way.

So, what are you waiting for? Dive in. You haven't got all day!

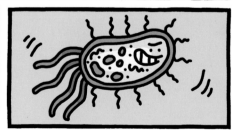

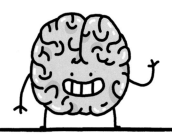

HUMAN BODY

Awake or asleep, running or resting – my goodness, you're always a busy body. That's what this section is all about: you and your insides. In fact, you could say it is packed full of 'inside information'. From the hairs on your head to the tips of your toes, get ready to bulge your brain with all you'll ever need to know about bogeys, bones, warts, wee, pimples, poo and a whole lot more. But be warned – for some of this stuff you may need a strong stomach. Luckily, you'll find one of those in these pages, too.

BRAIN

Hi. I'm your brain. I'm in charge of your body morning, noon and night.

Some say I'm a little bit controlling, but they're wrong ...

I'm 100% controlling! I run EVERYTHING. You've got me to thank when you're:

MOVING

THINKING

FEELING

I'm made up of billions of special cells* called neurons, which send and receive signals to and from everywhere in your body.

AXON TERMINAL

NUCLEUS

AXON

Neurons can send messages at hundreds of kilometres per hour. Together they could generate enough electricity to power a light bulb.

SHINE

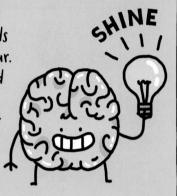

There are two halves to me, called hemispheres. In general, the left side of me controls the right side of your body, and the right controls the left.

RIGHT HEMISPHERE

LEFT HEMISPHERE

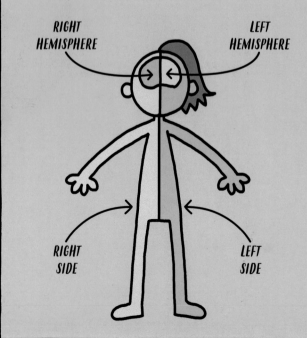

RIGHT SIDE

LEFT SIDE

And different parts of me do different jobs.

PLANNING AND PERSONALITY

TOUCH AND MOVEMENT

SIGHT

EMOTIONS AND MEMORY

CO-ORDINATION

There's lots of back and forth between me and different parts of the body. Maybe that's why I'm a bit clumsy sometimes!

OOPS!

*CELLS ARE THE BASIC BUILDING BLOCKS OF ALL LIFE

I do A LOT of work. I even keep going while you're asleep.

For instance, I lock away your memories of the day ...

CLICK!

... And I also turn off your muscles so that you can't act out your crazy dreams. Sorry!

If you prick your finger, pain receptors send a message up to the spinal cord.

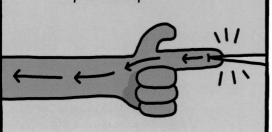

The spinal cord's reflex response makes you move immediately.

And I make a mental note for the future.

Must avoid sharp objects.

I also send chemical messages, called hormones, through your blood.

TO: LIVER

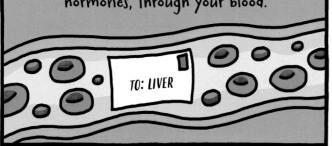

I am in touch with every bit of your body.

HEART   LIVER   TOES   BELLY BUTTON   BUM

Not bad for a soft, squishy, grey organ the size of a large grapefruit.

← 15 CM →   ← 15 CM →

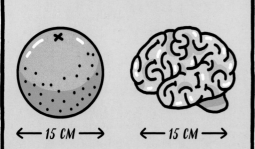

I may be controlling, but I do it all for you.

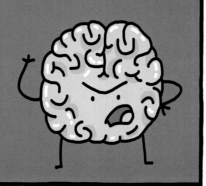

So please look after me.

DON'T GET ON A BIKE WITHOUT A HELMET!

EYE

I'm an eye – nice to see you.

My twin, Lefty, and I are part of your 'visual system', which allows you to see.

RIGHTY LEFTY

We receive information from the world around us and send it to the visual cortex at the back of your brain for processing.

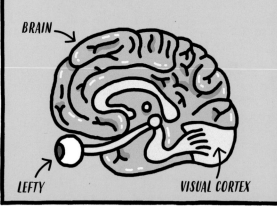

BRAIN

LEFTY VISUAL CORTEX

We're constantly on the move, whether it's scanning sentences like this one, or watching where you're going.

LOOKING RIGHT LOOKING LEFT LOOKING AT YOUR NOSE

Our 'pupils' – the black holes at the centre of us – change size constantly. They get larger or smaller depending on how much light there is.

NOT MUCH LIGHT: PUPILS GROW BIG TO LET MORE LIGHT IN.

LOTS OF LIGHT: PUPILS GET SMALL TO LET LESS LIGHT IN.

When light hits an eye, the lens focuses it on to a special layer of cells called the retina. However, this light is focused upside down, so it's sent to your brain to be processed the right way up.

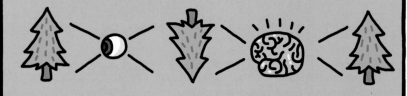

Even while you sleep, your eyes keep moving, especially during dreams.

THIS IS CALLED 'REM' (RAPID EYE MOVEMENT) SLEEP.

One thing eyes DON'T do is pop out when you sneeze. That's a myth. We'd never leave you like that.

GAHHH!

Looking at screens all day makes us tired. Why not read a book instead? Like this one!

Bye!

Eyes are complex structures with many important features. The average eye is 24 mm wide, around the size of a cherry tomato.

RETINA
This is a layer of special cells called rods and cones. They turn light into signals sent to the brain, via the optic nerve.

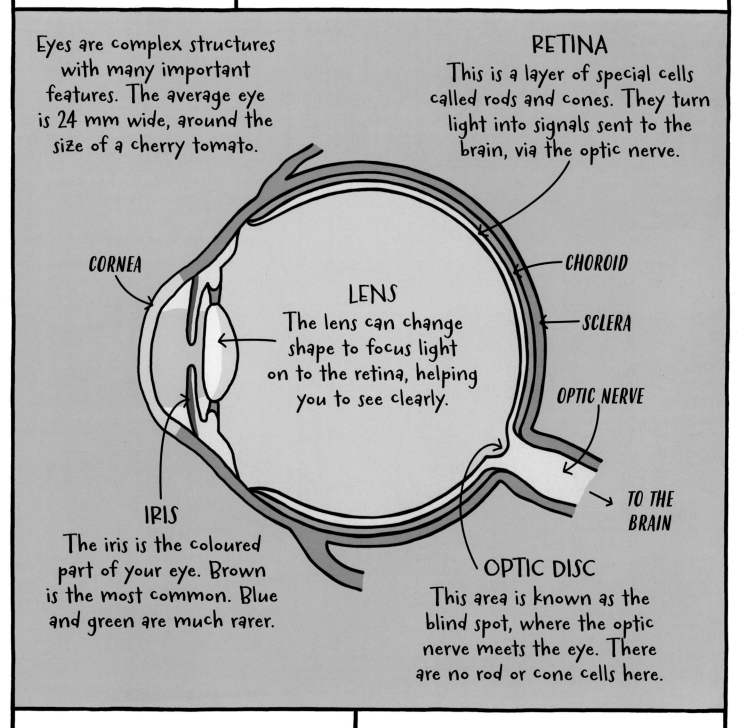

CORNEA

CHOROID

LENS
The lens can change shape to focus light on to the retina, helping you to see clearly.

SCLERA

OPTIC NERVE

TO THE BRAIN

IRIS
The iris is the coloured part of your eye. Brown is the most common. Blue and green are much rarer.

OPTIC DISC
This area is known as the blind spot, where the optic nerve meets the eye. There are no rod or cone cells here.

FIND YOUR BLIND SPOT
Close your left eye, then stare at the cross with your right eye. Move the page back and forwards until the eyeball 'vanishes'.

The secret diary of a
TOOTH

This extract comes from the diary of Mo, a 'molar' in the mouth of a ten-year-old girl.

Sparkle · Shine

MO

MONDAY

The day started with a good brush that left my outer layer of enamel sparkling clean. I'm told that tooth enamel is the hardest substance in the human body. The toothbrush still tickled a bit, though.

KEEP THOSE TEETH CLEAN!

PRE-MOLARS CRUSH AND GRIND

CANINES TEAR FOOD

INCISORS CUT AND CHOP FOOD

MOLARS MASH UP FOOD

TUESDAY

I found out the reason for all the deep-cleaning recently: school photo day. Because I'm right at the back, you can't see me very well. But that's OK, I don't like to be centre of attention, not like those show-off incisors.

WEDNESDAY

We went to the dentist today – it was funny seeing myself in the mirror she put inside the mouth. But what came next was even funnier: we had our pictures taken AGAIN, this time by an X-ray machine. I got to look at myself outside and in today – weird!

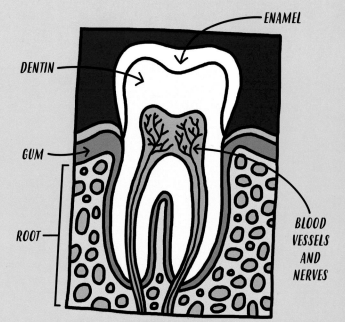

ENAMEL

DENTIN

GUM

ROOT

BLOOD VESSELS AND NERVES

THURSDAY

Back to the daily grind – literally. We had corn-on-the-cob for dinner. The incisors cut the kernels – the yellow bits – then us molars ground them up. It was good exercise, although afterwards one of the molars said he was feeling a bit wobbly. Uh-oh.

FRIDAY

Today we lost one of our pals – Morty the molar dropped out. But then, he was only a baby tooth and had to make way for permanent teeth. Our owner got a shiny coin in return – I hope she spends it on toothpaste.

shine!

TONGUE

Hi, I'm a human tongue. Let's talk.

I'm made of tough muscles that never stop working.

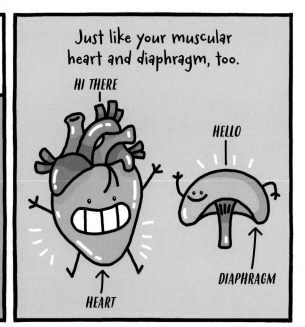

Just like your muscular heart and diaphragm, too.

HI THERE

HELLO

HEART

DIAPHRAGM

'Taste buds', which are special cells on my upper surface, can recognize five food tastes:

SWEET   SOUR   SALTY   BITTER   UMAMI (SAVOURY)

After chewing, I help shove food down your throat.

LOOK OUT BELOW!

I also let you speak. Without me there are very few words you can say. Some are good ones, though ...

BUM!

POP!

Some tongues even have super powers. Does yours?

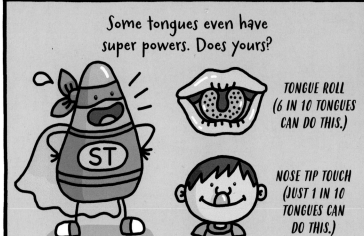

TONGUE ROLL (6 IN 10 TONGUES CAN DO THIS.)

NOSE TIP TOUCH (JUST 1 IN 10 TONGUES CAN DO THIS.)

At night, I get to relax a bit. Sadly, this sometimes means that saliva escapes out of your mouth. Oops!

SORRY ABOUT THAT — BYE!

HICCUP

Oh, hello. It's me, your ...

... HIC! ...

... diaphragm. I'm found here, in your upper abdomen, just below your lungs. Sorry about that hiccup. I had an ...

... HIC! ...

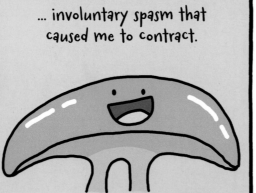

... involuntary spasm that caused me to contract.

This pulled air into your lungs, through your mouth.

AIR IN

Because it happened so fast, your vocal cords quickly closed shut.

OPEN   CLOSED

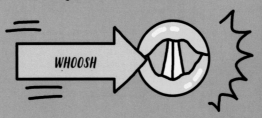

And when the air hit them, you got the classic sound ...

WHOOSH

HIC!

People claim there are lots of ways to cure hiccups, like:

DRINKING UPSIDE DOWN   HOLDING YOUR BREATH   GETTING A SHOCK

But really, you just have to wait. One man had hiccups for a record 68 years.

Charles Osborne (1894–1991)

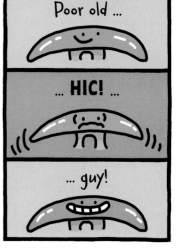

Poor old ...

... HIC! ...

... guy!

HAIR

Hey you! Come down here where you can take a look at me.

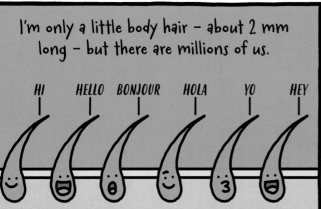

That's better. The bit you can see up top is actually dead.

Down here in the follicle is where all the growing happens.

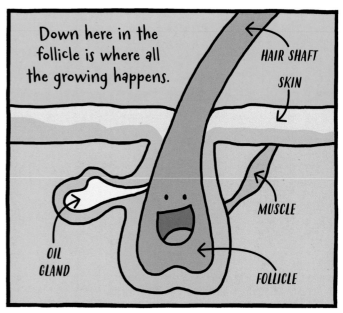

HAIR SHAFT

SKIN

MUSCLE

FOLLICLE

OIL GLAND

I'm only a little body hair — about 2 mm long — but there are millions of us.

HI   HELLO   BONJOUR   HOLA   YO   HEY

We help keep your skin the right temperature. Our muscles contract when it gets chilly ...

... which makes us rise up, trapping air between us, insulating your skin.

Our pals up on your head grow at a rate of about 15 cm a year.

FROM THIS ...   ... TO THIS

In some places, like your palms, the soles of your feet and on your lips, hair doesn't grow at all.

NOPE   NIL   NONE

Whereas, on some places it grows a lot.

THIS IS A GOOD LOOK FOR ME

Hair is made of 'keratin', a tough substance that also makes up your fingernails and the horns on a rhino.

LOOKIN' GOOD PAL

But, despite being made of strong stuff, all hairs fall out and are replaced eventually.

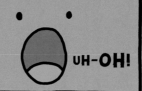

UH-OH!

ARGHHHH!

NITS AND PIECES

Sometimes, hair provides a home for unwanted guests, like head lice. They only live on humans and they love clean hair just as much as dirty hair. So, getting them is just a question of bad luck. They might be annoying, but they're completely harmless.

EGG CASE (NIT)

LOUSE

TASTY BLOOD, THANKS!

THE LIVES OF LICE
Lice live for about a month, with females laying anything from three to eight eggs per day. That's the bit known as a nit.

FEEDING TIME
Lice feed by sucking blood from your scalp until they glow red. They can't fly or jump, but they can crawl very quickly.

The secret diary of a
NOSE

This extract is from the diary of Norman, a nose belonging to a ten-year-old boy.

NORMAN

FIRST THING
The day began when my owner woke up and went to the loo – oh dear. I don't always get to smell lovely flowers and delicious food. My power of smell occurs when odour molecules from objects drift on the air, right on to my 'olfactory' (smell) receptors. So, there's nothing I can do to stop it.

NO THANKS

BETTER OUT THAN IN, YEAH?

8:45 am
My owner started sniffing and I began 'running'. It was partly my fault – the lining of my nostrils was making too much mucus. Most of it went down the back of me and my owner swallowed it (sorry, stomach). However, some of it ended up slipping out. Oops.

9:30 am

Small hairs inside my nostrils help stop dust and dirt making its way into the lungs when he breathes. After all that 'running', I started making the B-word: bogies! They occur when excess mucus in my nostrils dries out and clumps together.

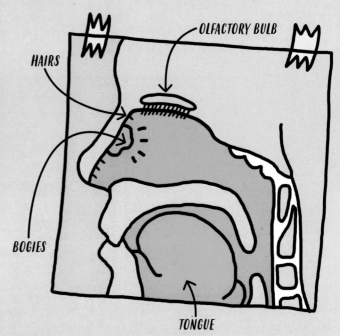

HAIRS

OLFACTORY BULB

BOGIES

TONGUE

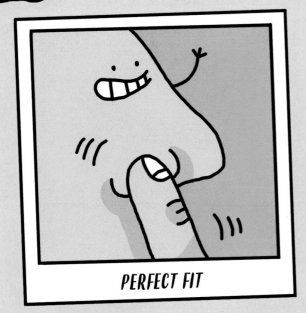

PERFECT FIT

9:45 am

Soon after, a finger came to visit. I know it's not exactly polite, but as my owner told his mum, "If we're not supposed to pick our noses, why are our fingers such a perfect fit?"

9:47 am

Urgh – I was hoping he'd roll it and flick it. Turns out he's a 'mucophage', a person who eats bogies. He swallowed it, dried mucus, hairs, dirt and all. Now, I'm just hoping he isn't a 'rhinotillexomaniac', someone who just can't stop picking their nose. I'll never be left alone.

THE SWALLOWED BOGEY

WART

Hi, I'm a wart. I don't have a great reputation. People HATE me.

But maybe after reading this I'll grow on you. Get it? Ha ha!

You can get warts anywhere on your skin. I'm a foot wart, known as a verruca. We're very common.

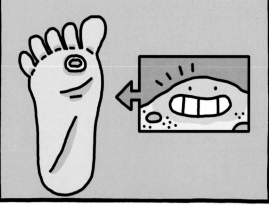

Common warts are caused by the 'human papilloma' virus, HPV, that infects your skin cells.

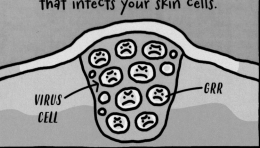

VIRUS CELL — GRR

Verrucas like me are caused by the same virus. I won't win any beauty contests, but I'm mostly harmless. And there are lots of ways to get rid of me – if you must.

CREAMS   LIQUID NITROGEN   MINOR SURGERY   PUMICE STONES

Fact is – and I shouldn't be telling you this – I'll probably just disappear naturally over time.

WILL YOU MISS ME?

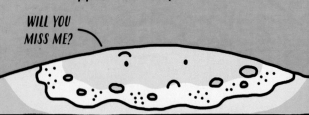

But luckily you humans keep helpfully passing us on, by picking at us and sharing the infection.

PICK =   SHAKE SHAKE

PICK

So, if you don't want a verruca like me for a best friend, never share towels, keep your feet dry, change your socks daily and wear flip flops if you go to the pool.

Maybe I shouldn't have told you that. It's a sad old life being walked on all day.

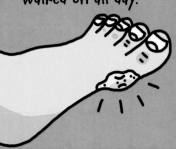

So catch me if you can, ha ha!

PIMPLE

Hi! I'm a pimple (a.k.a. a spot or a zit). I'm here to cause you trouble.

PIMPLE

SKIN

See? I've already grown bigger and more angry looking ... grrr!

In fact, at this rate, I'll soon be ready to burst with anger, and you don't want that. It's best not to touch me – it only makes me worse.

I form when pores (tiny holes) in your skin get blocked, trapping bacteria and oils inside them.

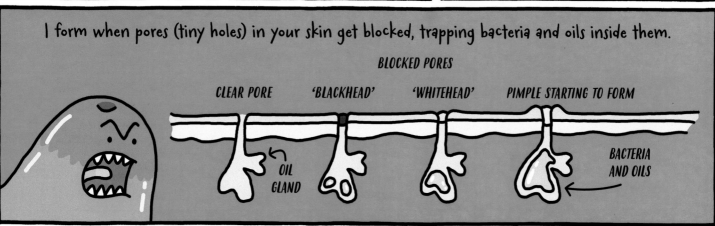

BLOCKED PORES

CLEAR PORE   'BLACKHEAD'   'WHITEHEAD'   PIMPLE STARTING TO FORM

OIL GLAND

BACTERIA AND OILS

The trapped bacteria form yellow pus, which causes the pimple to swell.

PUS

Pimples get red as your body fights back, by sending out white blood cells to combat the bacteria.

WHITE BLOOD CELL

BIFF!

BACTERIA

Really angry pimples are best left alone.

DON'T PUT ME UNDER PRESSURE!

Most pimples heal without treatment and anyone can get them – particularly teenagers.

PFFT! WHATEVER

So you might think you've got rid of me, but I'll see you again soon. Ha ha! Bye.

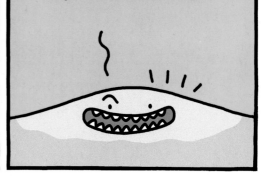

SKELETON

Hello, hello, hello. We're some of your bones.

SKULL AND JAW

SHOULDER BLADE

UPPER ARM

Shouldn't I be doing the talking round here?

BIG HEAD

We're part of your skeleton. There are 206 of us in an adult human.

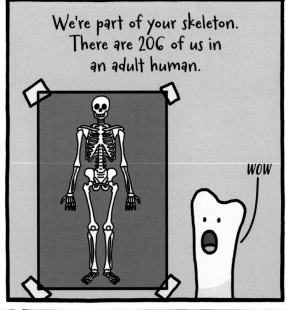

WOW

But newborns have more than 300. Some of those bones fuse together as you grow.

300 +

300 + 1 CHICKEN DRUMSTICK

The 'stapes' is the smallest bone in your body. It's found in the ear, where it helps to transmit sound waves.

IT'S ABOUT THE SIZE OF A GRAIN OF RICE.

The longest is the thigh bone, also known as the femur.

It's the hardest bone to break and is about a quarter of your height.

Your skeleton has a lot going on. Its five main functions are:

KEEPING YOUR BRAIN PROTECTED

KEEPING YOUR BODY UPRIGHT

HELPING YOU MOVE – HIGH FIVE!

MAKING BLOOD CELLS IN THE MARROW INSIDE US

STORING FAT AND MINERALS, SUCH AS CALCIUM

Your bones are all connected to each other by ligaments, muscles and tendons, like your elbow joint, here.

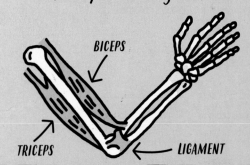

BICEPS

TRICEPS

LIGAMENT

Except for the hyoid bone. This bone, at the base of your tongue, isn't connected to any other.

I'M LONELY

So, as you can see, bones are very important.

WE COULD HAVE SAID ALL THAT

Bones make up around 20% of your body's weight. The heaviest and longest of them all is the femur, which is shown here.

COMPACT BONE
The shaft and outer layer of the the femur is made of 'compact bone', which is heavy and hard.

VEIN

ARTERY

BONE SHAFT

BLOOD SUPPLY

YELLOW MARROW
This is involved in the storage of fats and stem cells.

RED MARROW
This is where bones produce red and white blood cells, as well as 'platelets', tiny cells that help blood to 'clot' (thicken and dry) and form scabs when you have a cut or scratch.

CANCELLOUS BONE
This type of bone is spongy and is often found inside the end of long bones.

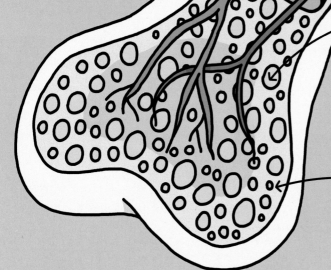

The secret diary of a
WHITE BLOOD CELL

This extract is from the diary of Phil, a type of white blood cell called a neutrophil.

PHIL

DAYS 1-7

I started off as a simple 'stem cell' (a cell that can turn into any other) inside your bone marrow. After seven days I matured into a neutrophil. It's the most common type, and it's my job to help you fight infections. Luckily, I'm not alone. There are about 100 billion of us created inside your body daily.

IT'S BUSY IN HERE!

I'M FREE!

DAY 8

At last! I left the marrow and entered the blood stream. Those red blood cells outnumbered us massively, but I was just happy to be moving.

DAY 8: 1 pm

Emergency! Bacteria got into a cut finger. The time came for us white blood cells to spring into action – my big moment.

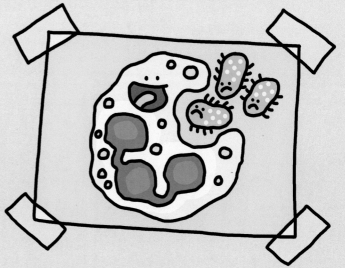

DAY 8: 2 pm

I was carried in the blood to the infected area. I began by engulfing the invaders, flowing my outer membrane around them and trapping them in little sacs inside me. GOTCHA!

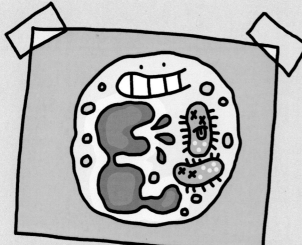

DAY 8: 3 pm

Next came the fun bit. I released special enzymes* into the sacs containing the bacteria, destroying them. Victory!

DAY 8: 4 pm

Now it's time for me to say goodbye, too. Neutrophils only last a few hours. Soon I'll be removed by a 'macrophage' – a fellow white blood cell that gets rid of dead cells. Oh well, I did my bit!

NOM!

*CHEMICAL SUBSTANCES THAT SPEED UP REACTIONS IN THE BODY

LUNGS

Hi! I'm your right lung.

And I'm your left lung.

That thing in between us is our 'trachea', or 'windpipe'.

Left lungs are always a little bit smaller to leave room for your heart.

AW, THANKS PAL

We're made of soft, spongy tissue, full of air spaces. We're so light we could float in water. (Not that we tend to do that.)

FANCY A SWIM?

Together, we bring oxygen into your body and send carbon dioxide out.

O_2 IN

CO_2 OUT

And we never stop, even when you sleep.

IT'S AMAZING WHAT YOU SEE AT NIGHT.

We take about 25,000 breaths each day. That's a lot of balloons we could blow up.

When you breathe in, your ribs move up and out, and the diaphragm contracts, moving down. This action fills us with air.

O_2 IN

RIBS

DIAPHRAGM DOWN

When you breathe out, your ribs move down and in, the diaphragm relaxes and moves up, pushing air back out.

CO_2 OUT

RIBS

DIAPHRAGM UP

And all this happens without you needing to think about it.

WE'RE SO SMART

Still, you can control how you breathe and even hold your breath.

But we don't like that, so please don't.

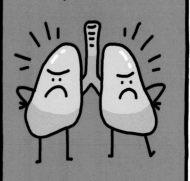

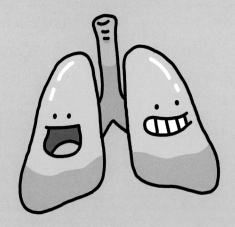

See how amazing we are? You could even say we're breath-taking. Ha! So, remember to exercise and take care of us, so we get stronger and more efficient.

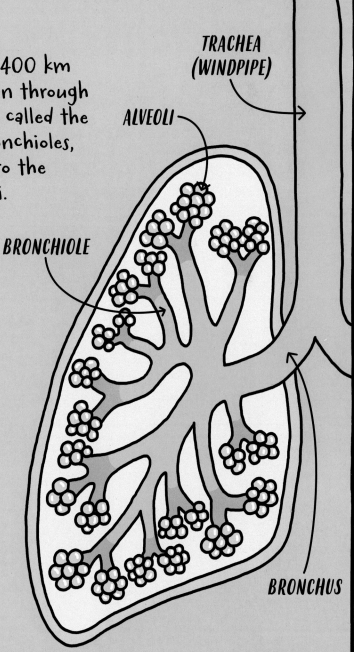

TRACHEA (WINDPIPE)

ALVEOLI

BRONCHIOLE

BRONCHUS

AIRWAYS

The lungs contain 2,400 km of airways. Air travels in through the trachea, into tubes called the bronchus and the bronchioles, and eventually into the sac-like alveoli.

ALVEOLI

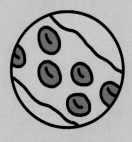

At the alveoli, red blood cells pick up oxygen and release carbon dioxide, to be breathed out.

CILIA

CILIA

Some of the airways are lined with mucus and 'cilia', tiny hairs that trap dirt and germs before moving them up and out.

HEART

I'm a human heart, and I'm PUMPED!

I ♥ my job!

I was the first organ formed in your body. I've been beating away since before you were born.

SO COSY

You can find me in your chest, just between the lungs. I pump blood around your body all day long – so it's a good job I'm made of tough, muscular tissue.

SURE, I WORK OUT

I send blood on a 19,000 km journey all around your body each and every day – just short of the distance from London to Tokyo and back.

 → → →  →

FROM ME *TO THE LUNGS* *BACK TO ME* *THEN EVERYWHERE YOU CAN THINK OF* *AND BACK TO ME AGAIN*

Not bad for an organ about the size of your fist.

My beat is controlled by an electrical signal sent by a group of cells called the sinoartrial node.

When you're resting, I beat around 60-100 times per minute.

KEEP THAT BEAT!

Each beat contains the same force needed to squash a tennis ball.

THAT'S ACE

I have to keep pretty fit to do all this, so stay active and healthy.

LET'S GO!

In the time you've taken to read this page, I've done around another hundred squeezes. See, I never stop.

The human circulatory system is a network of tubes called blood vessels that pump blood around your whole body. I'm at its, erm, heart.

AORTA
This is the biggest 'artery' – a tube that carries blood with oxygen in it – in the body. It carries blood away from the heart.

PERFECT 'PLUMBING'
The heart has four chambers, known as ventricles and atria, as well as a number of valves that stop blood flowing backwards.

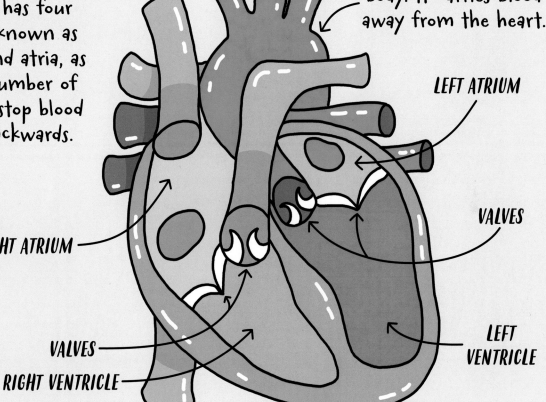

LEFT ATRIUM

VALVES

RIGHT ATRIUM

LEFT VENTRICLE

VALVES

RIGHT VENTRICLE

INFERIOR VENA CAVA
This is the largest 'vein' – a tube that carries oxygen-depleted blood – in your body. It returns blood from your lower half.

LONG DISTANCE
Including all the very narrow vessels called capilliaries, there are over 96,000 km of blood vessels in the body, which is more than twice the distance around the Earth.

STOMACH

Hungry for some information about your stomach?

Well, I'm a bag-like, muscular organ located between your oesophagus and small intestine.

IT'S TRUE

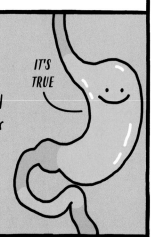

You could say I'm your very own 'bag for life'. I'm important for your digestive system – the process of breaking down and absorbing food.

FEED ME!

When chewed food enters me, a ring of muscle, called a sphincter, clamps shut.

SPHINCTER

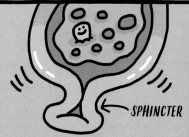

SPHINCTER

There's also one at the other end. They stop food escaping.

When I'm empty, I'm flat, but once you fill me up I can really expand.

BULGE

I squash and squeeze your food, mixing it with special chemicals called enzymes.

SQUISH
SQUELCH
SQUEEZE

I also add a substance called hydrochloric acid. It's so strong it can clean the rust off steel.

SCRUB SCRUB

This creates a semi-liquid mass of partially digested food called chyme.

EWW

Chyme then goes on to the small intestine, unless something bad irritates my lining.

BRAIN HERE – SOMETHING'S NOT RIGHT

In that case, the diaphragm and abdominal muscles contract, increasing the pressure on me and forcing food out.

BARF!

It's all in a day's work for me. (By the way, what's for dinner?)

FEED ME!

A DAY IN THE LIFE OF A ...

LIVER

Look, I'm very busy, so let's make this quick. Got any idea what I do? For your information, I do pretty much EVERYTHING!

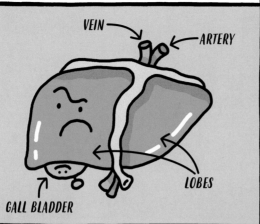

VEIN

ARTERY

LOBES

GALL BLADDER

At least, that's what it feels like. I have loads of different jobs to do, all the time, every day. There's no time to lose!

GO GO GO!

Yet, even though I'm important, most people don't even know where I am.

SORRY

I'm HERE, in the upper abdomen, just below your diaphragm.

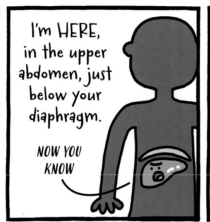

NOW YOU KNOW

I'm the biggest gland and heaviest organ in the body, weighing about 1.5 kg.

LOSERS

I may not be full of joy, but just look at all the jobs I have to do:

CLEANING BLOOD

STORING VITAMINS AND MINERALS

REMOVING TOXINS

MAKING BILE ...

... WHICH I STORE

I also make hormones, proteins, fight infections ... the list goes on and on.

- Make dinner
- Walk the dog
- Feed the goldfish

The energy I create warms the blood passing through me, helping maintain your body temperature, too.

THANKS

Yet everyone just LOVES the heart. What did that guy ever do?

HEY!

I just want to be loved, too.

SOB

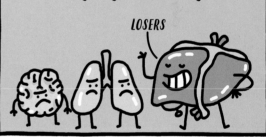

BLADDER

Hi! I'm your bladder. I've been BURSTING to talk to you.

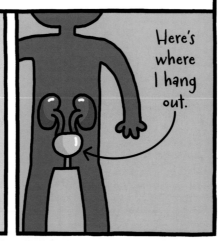

Here's where I hang out.

I'm basically a bag of muscles, about the size and shape of an upside-down pear.

¿NO GOING ON? WHAT'S

The liquid you drink is filtered by the kidneys, which keep the good stuff you need and pass the waste product, urine, on to me. I hold on to it for a bit, until it's got rid of via the urethra.

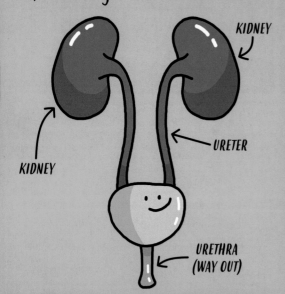

KIDNEY

KIDNEY

URETER

URETHRA (WAY OUT)

Over time, I get more and more filled up, growing bigger and bigger and BIGGER.

UH-OH

I can hold about 400–500 ml of liquid, but after 350 ml things get very uncomfortable. Luckily, your brain is on hand to tell me what to do.

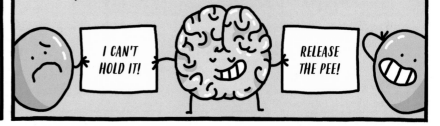

I CAN'T HOLD IT!

RELEASE THE PEE!

Bigger kids can train their brains to fight the urge, using muscles to stop the flow. Babies are not so clever.

WAHHHHH

Even so, when you've gotta go, you've gotta go ...

GET READY!

Ahh, that's better.

PHEW!

Now wash your hands!

Did you know, 96% of urine is made up of water? The rest is salts and 'urea', a waste product from the breakdown and absorbtion of protein in your body. If you liked that fact, I know you'll be DESPERATE for more.

YUCK!

Some food and drink can make your pee pong. Asparagus adds a strong scent to most people's wee, although not everyone can smell this. Coffee can make it smell, too, as well as foods rich in vitamin B6, such as bananas.

In the past, wee was collected and combinbed with straw, manure and leaves to make 'saltpetre', a substance that was vital for the creation of gunpowder. Explosive wee? Who would've thought it?

YIKES

YOU'RE TAKING A SUSPICIOUSLY LONG TIME

Did you know that most mammals larger than rats wee for around 20 seconds, even elephants, and that a single elephant can wee up to 9 litres at a time? Oh, and cat urine glows in the dark under ultraviolet light! Isn't weeing a wonderful thing?

INTESTINES

If I stay any longer I'll start getting wrinkly – he he. As you can see, the rest of your dinner has turned into a gloopy substance called chyme*.

Over here! I'm a piece of sweetcorn just about to leave your stomach. I've been in here over an hour.

Now I'm just waiting to go with it on the greatest ride known to food-kind ...

DON'T FORGET ME, TOO

... Also known as the journey through your intestines. Here's a handy map of where I've been and where I'm going.

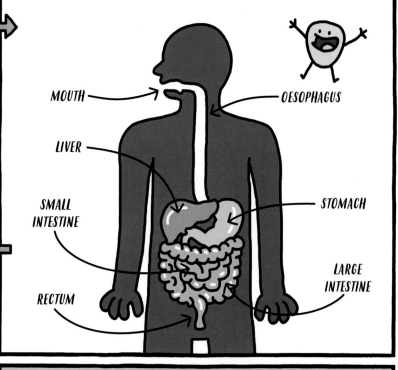

MOUTH

OESOPHAGUS

LIVER

SMALL INTESTINE

STOMACH

RECTUM

LARGE INTESTINE

Food leaves the stomach through a special muscular valve called the pyloric sphincter.

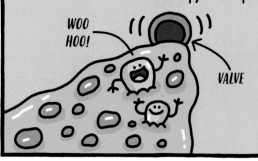

WOO HOO!

VALVE

First stop is the small intestine. It might only be 2.5 cm wide, but it's around 6–8 m long.

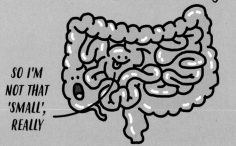

SO I'M NOT THAT 'SMALL', REALLY

Me and the chyme get squeezed along by waves of muscular contractions. These waves are known as peristalsis.

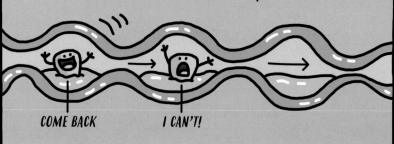

COME BACK

I CAN'T!

*SEE STOMACH ON PAGE 30

Along the way we get covered in bile from the gall bladder and enzymes from your pancreas.

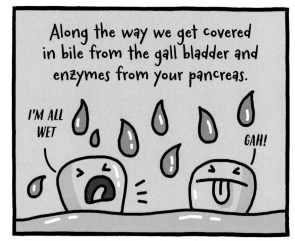

Bile makes chyme less acidic after that trip through your stomach, and enzymes break down fat and protein. To be honest, all these liquids are a bit icky.

MUST GET CLEAN

After that, the nutrients in your food are absorbed through millions of tiny 'fingers' called villi, which line the walls of your intestines.

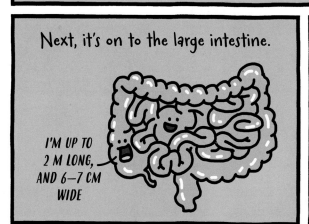

THEY'RE WAVING AT ME

If you stretched out your small intestine, including villi, it would have almost the same surface area as a badminton court.

FUN!

Next, it's on to the large intestine.

I'M UP TO 2 M LONG, AND 6–7 CM WIDE

Here, bacteria help retrieve more of the remaining goodness from your food. Water is absorbed into your body, too.

BACTERIA

I FEEL DIRTY

I'M PARCHED

The final part of the large intestine is the rectum. This is where any remaining nutrients are absorbed, and what's left is smushed together to become poo. Here, it waits to be pooped out of the anus.

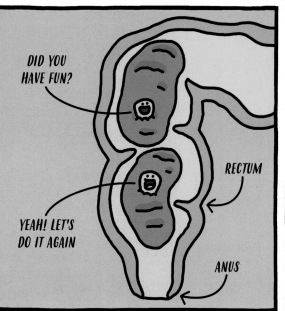

DID YOU HAVE FUN?

YEAH! LET'S DO IT AGAIN

RECTUM

ANUS

And a new journey begins ...

FLUSH!

A DAY IN THE LIFE OF A ...

POO

What a day I've had. It's all go when you're a poo.

First I got flushed ...

... And I went on the ride of my short life.

WOO HOO

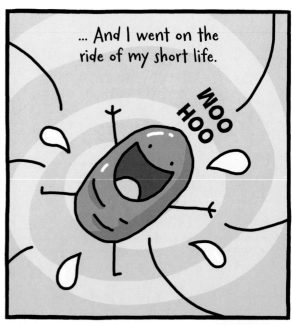

After that, your wee and I, as well as lots of other poos, flowed through a series of pipes into a massive sewer.

IT'S A POO PARTY

The sewer led to a waste water treatment plant ...

... Where we were squished through a series of sieves ...

... Turning all of us poos into sludge.

WHAT A WILD RIDE!

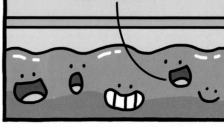

The sludge was then sent to be broken down by special bacteria.

IT'S NOT THE BEST JOB EVER, BUT I DON'T MIND

Some of it was turned into fertilizer* for crops.

Which can go into growing new food. Cool, eh?

SMELL YA LATER ...

*FERTILIZER IS A SUBSTANCE ADDED TO SOIL OR LAND TO HELP PLANTS GROW

Poos can give you a clue as to what's going on inside your gut. Hard poos are a symptom of 'constipation' – that's when you find it difficult to go. Runny poos are a sign of 'diarrhoea' – that's when you can't stop going. Why not check your poos against these poos below and find out what they mean?

SMALL, HARD LUMPS
Very constipated, can be painful.

LUMPY SAUSAGE
Mild constipation. Eat more veggies and drink more water.

CRACKED SAUSAGE
This is a good poo. Well done, keep up the good work.

SMOOTH SAUSAGE
Another good poo. You're a poo champ!

SOFT BLOBS
More fibre needed in your diet, this is a loose poo.

MUSHY STUFF
Mild diarrhoea. You might be ill.

LIQUID POO
DANGER! It's the poo of nightmares.

FART

I'm a fart, also known as a:

TRUMP
BOTTOM BURP
RASPBERRY
TOOT
PARP
SQUEAKY
BOMB

Well, I will be if I ever get out of your bum. Right now I'm trapped wind.

I'm here, in your colon, which is part of your large intestine. Just hanging out with my pals.

WANT TO HEAR A POO JOKE?

NAH, THEY ALWAYS STINK

Lots of what made me is just air you accidentally swallowed. A quarter of me is made up of oxygen and nitrogen.

GULP

AIR

Some of me is made up of carbon dioxide, which is made when stomach acid breaks down food.

FIZZ

FIZZ

But the really interesting – and smelly – stuff is made here among the poop.

TELL US MORE

Microbes* feed on undigested food and create smelly hydrogen sulphide ...

BLOOP!

... That's the gas that really whiffs. Beware certain foods, some of them have more fart-producing qualities than others, such as:

BEANS   BROCCOLI   CABBAGE   RADISHES   BRUSSELS SPROUTS

Everyone farts, especially when they sleep.

URGH, WHY?

PARP!

The sound comes from your anal muscles vibrating and – amazingly – most farts are odourless.

WAY OUT!

Sadly, not this one.

EWWW GROSS

PRRRRPPPP!

*MICROBES ARE TINY LIVING THINGS MADE UP OF A SMALL NUMBER OF CELLS

 **A DAY IN THE LIFE OF A ...**

COUGH

Don't mind me, I'm just a teeny, tiny speck of dust. Pretty harmless, right?

WRONG. I can be incredibly irritating.

Just like bacteria, germs and smoke, I can cause you to cough. And you never know when I'm going to strike.

OBLIVIOUS

First, a gust of wind sends me rushing into your mouth.

HERE I GO

... and straight into your windpipe.

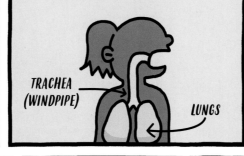

TRACHEA (WINDPIPE)

LUNGS

This is the start of the 'cough reflex'.

HUH?

When I hit the side of the trachea, nerve endings alert the rest of the body.

DING DING DING DING

Your lungs spring into action, taking a deep breath.

Your vocal cords snap shut, so no air can escape.

OPEN   CLOSED

Finally, your lungs push that air against the cords, forcing them open very quickly.

COUGH

That explosive action is a cough, and it pushes me out at about 160 km/h.

WHEEEE

And I'm free to roam the air again, waiting for my next victim. Mwa ha ha ha!

HAND

We're team hand. Give us a wave.

I'm thumb, the most independent member of the team.

HOWDY

That's because I'm 'opposable', which means I can move to face and touch the fingers.

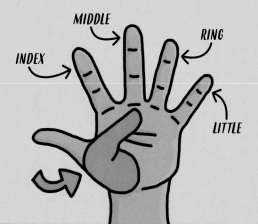

MIDDLE

RING

INDEX

LITTLE

Being opposable is useful because it allows you to grip things.

'Handy', right?

HA!

Did you know: if you touch your thumb to your little finger, you might see a thin tendon* in your wrist? Around 85–90% of people have this.

'PALMARIS LONGUS'

This tendon isn't handy at all. It's 'vestigial', which means that it's left over from our distant past when it was needed for moving through the trees. Some monkeys and lemurs still use this today, though.

YES, WE KNOW

THUMB WAR?

Team hand also includes:

FINGERNAILS THAT PROTECT THE ENDS OF YOUR FINGERS

PALMS, WHICH HOLD THINGS AND ARE COMPLETELY HAIRLESS

'PAPILLARY RIDGES' — FINGERPRINTS. THEY GRIP THINGS AND ARE UNIQUE IN EVERY HUMAN

So you see, there's nothing quite like your hand ... Except for your other one, of course. Ha!

*A TENDON IS A FLEXIBLE CORD OF TISSUE

A DAY IN THE LIFE OF A ...
FOOT

We're team foot.

WALK THIS WAY!

Let me tell you where we stand.

ON THE GROUND?

Here you can see the important elements that make up our team:

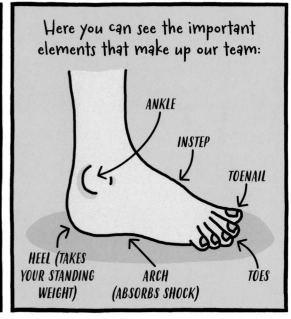

ANKLE

INSTEP

TOENAIL

HEEL (TAKES YOUR STANDING WEIGHT)

ARCH (ABSORBS SHOCK)

TOES

And we also have 26 bones inside that you can't see.

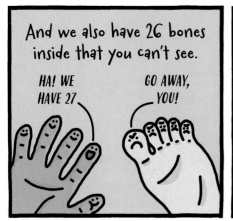

HA! WE HAVE 27

GO AWAY, YOU!

Some people have a second toe that's longer than the big one, a condition called Morton's toe.

BEAT YA!

And some people are born with an extra toe – a condition called polydactylism.

ROOM FOR A SMALL ONE?

Humans are 'bipedal'. This means that you use two feet instead of four to walk around. We're not the only ones, though. Other primates* do sometimes, too.

When we hit the ground, the 'Achilles tendon' stretches. Then, when we push off again, it releases energy, helping us on our way.

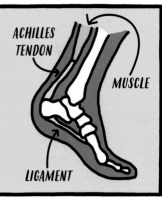

ACHILLES TENDON

MUSCLE

LIGAMENT

Luckily, it's not all walk, walk, walk. There's a fun side to us, too. With over 100,000 nerve endings per foot, we're very ticklish.

NO! STOP IT!

One foot has around 125,000 sweat glands, producing about a cup's worth of sweat each day.

I WOULDN'T DRINK THIS IF I WERE YOU

It's lucky we're such a close team; we spend a lot of time together!

COSY IN HERE!

---

*PRIMATES ARE MAMMALS THAT INCLUDE HUMANS, MONKEYS AND APES

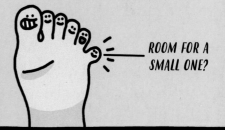

The secret diary of a
RED BLOOD CELL

This extract is from the diary of Rusty, a red blood cell. (Also known as an erythrocyte.)

RUSTY

WEEK ONE

Just seven days ago I was a simple stem cell in the marrow of a bone, until I finally became a red blood cell. Woo hoo! I might be microscopic, but a human has more than 20 trillion copies of me. Pretty cool, huh?

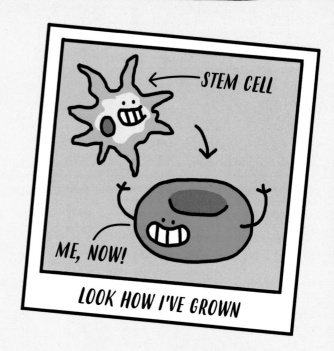
STEM CELL
ME, NOW!
LOOK HOW I'VE GROWN

PLATELET

WHITE BLOOD CELL

ME WITH OXYGEN

ME WITHOUT OXYGEN

WEEK TWO

Out in the bloodstream there were also 'platelets' – tiny blood cells that stop bleeding – white blood cells and many more red blood cells, too. My job is to pick up oxygen in the lungs, carry it to tissues, pick up waste carbon dioxide, and take it back to the lungs to be breathed out.

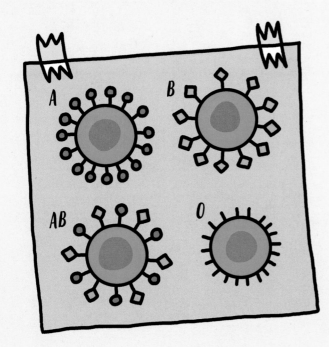

WEEK FIVE

People have different blood groups. The four main blood groups are A, B, O and AB. Which group you have depends on 'antigens', special markers that help your body identify blood cells that don't belong to you.

WEEK TEN

Today I saw an old red blood cell being engulfed by a white blood cell. This happens to all of us after about four months. Oh well, a new red blood cell will take its place – two million are made every second.

WEEK TWELVE

What an adventure! I was just travelling along an arm when I was diverted outside, down a tube and into a bag, which is now in a hospital fridge. Our owner donates blood. It will be used to help a new person get well again, as long as our blood groups are compatible.

JUST SAVING LIVES!

CELL MATES

Humans have around 30 trillion cells. There are about 200 different types, each with their own special job to do. You'd need a microscope to see most of them – luckily there's one here.

FAT CELLS

These are also known as lipocytes. They store fat, which you can later burn as energy.

DID SOMEONE SAY 'BURN'?

CONE CELLS

You'll find cone cells in the retinas, at the back of your eyes. They are responsible for colour vision.

NICE TO SEE YOU!

SKIN CELLS

The outer layer of your skin is called the epidermis. It forms the boundary between your body and the outside world. Dead skin cells rise to the top and flake off.

MUSCLE CELLS

These cells can stretch and contract to allow your muscles to produce force and movement.

WE'RE SO STRONG!

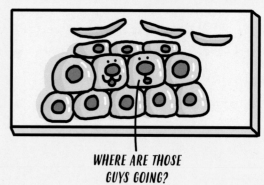

WHERE ARE THOSE GUYS GOING?

ANIMAL KINGDOM

Growl! Roar! Hiss! Squeak! This section could well bring out the beast in you: it's all about animals. Whether they creep, crawl, walk, fly, flap or swim, a whole host of animals are about to reveal their life stories. So, if you've ever wanted to hang with a bat, roll with a pangolin or dig the dirt on a dung beetle, turn the page quickly. You're in for a whale of a time ... Literally!

MAYFLY

Hello! I'm a male mayfly, named after the month.

THERE'S A MONTH CALLED 'FLY'?

No, May. Buzz off, this is my story.

CHARMING!

People think mayflies like me only live for one day. We do have short lives, but that's not the whole story.

JULY 13

My life began when my mum laid an egg. After two weeks, I hatched into my 'nymph' stage.

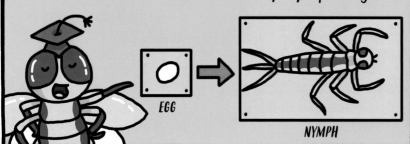

EGG

NYMPH

As a nymph, I lived under a rock eating algae. Those were the days. Now I'm grown up, I don't eat anything.

SO HUNGRY ...

I was a nymph for about a year, then I transformed. The skin down my back split, and my wings emerged. This was my 'subimago' stage.

WOO HOO! NOW I CAN FLY

SUBIMAGO

That only lasted a day, after which I shed my skin again to become an adult 'imago'. Now it's time to find a mate.

IMAGO

HELLO

WRONG TYPE OF INSECT, PAL

Hopefully my mid-air dancing skills will attract a female in the end.

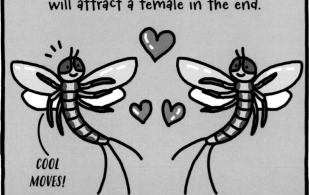

COOL MOVES!

Then, she'll lay eggs in the water, and the cycle will start all over again.

NOT IF I EAT YOU FIRST

We're only adults for hours or even minutes. And here I am talking to you!

WHY?

BEE

Welcome to the hive. I'm a western honey bee. This place is buzzin'.

I'm a worker bee, one of those that fetch all the pollen and nectar from flowers to make honey.

There are thousands of us workers, working hard for the hive all day long. We're all females, AND sisters.

WE'RE THE BIG SISTERS

WE'RE THE SAME AGE, SILLY

We each hatched from eggs laid by our queen, the leader of the hive.

CALL ME 'YOUR MAJESTY'

CAN'T WE CALL YOU 'MUM'?

And there's also a small number of male bees, known as drones.

HEY!

But their only job is to mate with the queen, after which they die.

GULP!

SORRY ABOUT THAT

After mating, her royal honeyness lays eggs in the nest's honeycomb cells. That's how I was born.

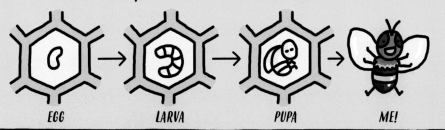

EGG → LARVA → PUPA → ME!

My first job was cleaning the hive, making honey and looking after the larvae.

WHO'S A PRETTY LARVA?

Until finally, I got to fly outside and visit some flowers.

LUCKY ME

I can fly up to 800 km and visit thousands of flowers in my lifetime.

I'M A BUSY BEE

But it's raining today, so I'm staying in to put my feet up. See you around.

The secret diary of a
SLUG

This extract is from the diary of Sam, a black slug living in a back garden.

SAM

MONDAY

Glorious weather today – constant rain. There's nothing slugs love more than a dark, damp night. Moisture is the BEST – without it, my nice thick layer of slime might dry out. My slime allows me to slither around, and it makes it more difficult for predators to grab me.

I ♥ THE RAIN

THE ENEMY

TUESDAY

I bumped into a stupid snail while following an old slime trail today. Just because he has a shell, he started teasing me about not having my own home. Fat lot of good it does him. Snails have to hibernate in winter, but slugs don't. What a loser.

WEDNESDAY

Thought I'd go for a 'run' today. Didn't get very far, though – my top speed is about 2–3 metres per hour. I'm what's known as a 'gastropod', which comes from the Greek words for 'stomach' and 'foot'. However, that has nothing to do with my running abilities. I'm called that because my muscular 'foot' is below my belly.

I HATE 'RUNNING'

MY RADULA

THURSDAY

DISASTER! I got some food stuck in my teeth. Honestly, though, it happens a lot. I do have about 27,000 of them. They're on my 'radula'. This is a horny, ribbon-like structure inside my mouth, which is what I use to chomp through all sorts of delicious dinner. I'll eat vegetation, fungi, earthworms, decaying animal remains and even dung. Mmm.

FRIDAY

When it comes to reproducing, I have both male and female reproductive organs. When I find a mate, we fertilize each other's eggs, but then go our separate ways. So, now I have a night in with my favourite slug – me! Oh, and the 150 fertilized eggs I'm about to lay.

ME AND MY EGGS

SPIGER

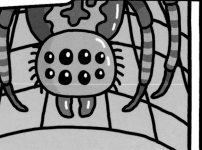

I've got my eyes on you. All eight of them, actually.

Don't panic, though, I'm just quietly passing the day on my web.

I'm a female garden spider, a type of 'orb weaver'. As you can see, I'm a great web spinner.

There's about 20 m of silk in one of my webs, dontcha know?

I make the web structure with regular silk and I add the sticky glue later.

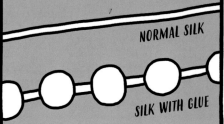

NORMAL SILK

SILK WITH GLUE

It only takes an hour to spin, is designed to catch bees and flies, and it all comes out of organs called spinnerets.

HERE THEY ARE!

Can your bum do that?

Now I'm just waiting for flies to get stuck on the sticky silk. This is the boring part.

Here's some I caught earlier, wrapped up in silk.

TWANG!

Ooh! I wonder who that is.

Oh, it's only a male, looking for a mate.

HELLO!

YOU LOOK TASTY

Literally. I don't want a boyfriend, but I am hungry. He'll do for dinner!

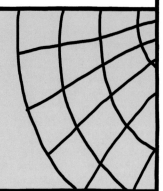

Spiders are from a class of animals called arachnids, which also includes scorpions, ticks and mites. Different spiders have very different days. Check out these unusual eight-legged pals of mine.

DIVING BELL

Diving bell spiders are the underwater adventurers of the spider kingdom. They spend almost their entire lives underwater in bubbles of air they keep trapped under their silk.

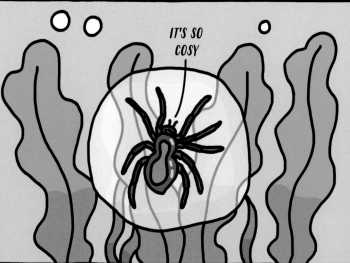

IT'S SO COSY

DON'T MIND ME, NOTHING TO SEE HERE

BUZZ OFF!

NET-CASTING

Net-casting spiders take web-making skills to the next level. They create webs that they hold in their front legs, ready to stretch out and catch unsuspecting prey as it goes by.

TRAPDOOR

Trapdoor spiders build burrows with hinged lids on them made of soil or plant debris. Then, they hide in the ground before springing out to surprise their prey.

WHERE DID THAT COME FROM?

The secret diary of an
EARTHWORM

This extract is from the diary of Whitney, an earthworm living under a garden lawn in Europe.

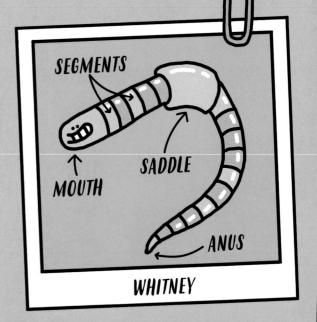

SEGMENTS

MOUTH

SADDLE

ANUS

WHITNEY

MONDAY

I'm writing this in my burrow under the lawn before heading up top tonight. I sensed the vibrations of raindrops thudding on the grass earlier, so I know it will be lovely and wet up there. Looking forward to feasting on dead leaves – yum!

HOME SWEET HOME

TUESDAY

Well, what a night it was. I was chomping on a nice old oak leaf, half in, half out of my burrow, when suddenly, footsteps! A sneaky fox tried to make me its supper. Luckily, I pulled myself back down into my burrow just in time. You could say I outfoxed him.

WEDNESDAY

More mammal troubles! Today I had a mole in my hole. I could sense it burrowing towards me so this time I fled upwards, fast. It was all very scary – good job worm poo is good for the soil.

THURSDAY

I've found myself a partner. A worm can be both male and female, and we will each be laying lots of little eggs in the near future.

FRIDAY

OUCH! I got chopped in half by a spade today while I was minding my own business. I miss my wiggly tail, which will die, but at least I can grow a new one. Still, it's unlikely I'll ever beat the world record for the longest ever earthworm, which stands at an amazing 61 cm.

DUNG BEETLE

Pleased to meet you! I'm a male dung beetle, and I'm just rolling with it ...

... Dung, that is. I got me a BIG ball.

Well, it belongs to me and my partner, actually. Pure elephant poop, it is. Some of us dung beetles can roll balls up to 50 times our own body weight.

PUSH!
KICK!
SHOVE!

THIS IS A FUN RIDE

We just love poo. We live it, breathe it and, in fact, it's the only thing we eat.

CHOMP
CHOMP
CHOMP

THIS ONE'S DELICIOUS

But you've got to be careful no one steals your stash.

SHOVE OFF!

RUDE

Sadly, some dung beetles just have no manners.

No matter what gets in the way, we push this old poo ball in a straight line. We're the only invertebrates* to navigate by using the Sun, the Moon and the Milky Way.

CLEVER

Eventually, we dig a hole and bury the dung ball inside.

But not before my partner has laid her eggs in it. When they hatch into 'grubs' they'll eat the dung, too.

SO PROUD OF THEM!

Our work is literally a pile of poo, but at least the ancient Egyptians thought we were sacred.

I COULD GET USED TO THIS

*AN INVERTEBRATE IS A CREATURE WITHOUT A BACKBONE

LIMPET

Hello, I'm a limpet, one of the clingiest things alive. Here's me in a rock pool. Just rockin' out – he he.

I can't show you my face because ...
I HAVEN'T GOT ONE!

GASP!

Other 'molluscs'*, such as snails and slugs, do, but not me.

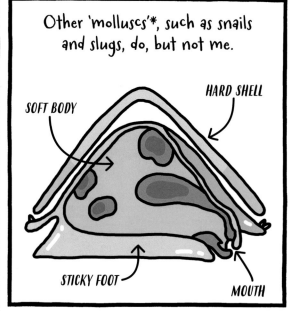

SOFT BODY

HARD SHELL

STICKY FOOT

MOUTH

I cling to rocks until the tide comes in, so that I don't dry out.

ALMOST THERE

HURRY UP

Once under the sea, I'm off on my muscular foot in search of food.

ZOOM!

I feed by scraping algae off rocks, leaving a trail of mucus behind as I go.

YUCK

NOM NOM

My tongue has more than 100 rows of tiny teeth made up of very small fibres. These fibres consist of an iron-based mineral called geothite. It's the strongest known biological material.

COMING TO GET YA ...

TAKE YOUR TIME

Sadly, some critters, such as starfish, find us quite tasty. Time to hide under my shell.

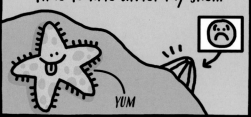

YUM

Some limpets can change from male to female. Scientists think that it happens when there's a lack of females in the population.

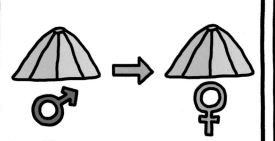

Before the tide disappears, we follow our mucus trails back to the exact spot we started from.

JUST IN TIME

So, it's just as well I get on with the neighbours.

THAT'S WHAT HE THINKS!

*A MOLLUSC IS A TYPE OF INVERTEBRATE ANIMAL WITH A SOFT BODY AND SOMETIMES A HARD SHELL

SEA JELLY

Scientists now prefer to call me a sea jelly, because we are NOT fish. Moon jellies like me are found in oceans worldwide and can be up to 40 cm in diameter.

I'm a jellyfish, right?

PULSE   SWIM

WRONG!

ORAL ARM

TENTACLES   BELL

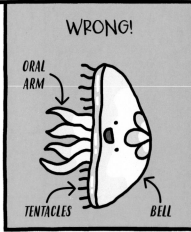

Personally, I don't mind what I'm called, or which way up I am ...

THAT'S NO FISH !

But then I have no brain, heart or lungs.

PFFT

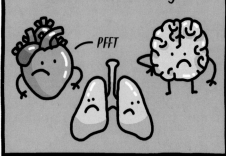

I swim by contracting my muscles, bringing water into my bell, then pushing it out again – a form of jet propulsion!

WHEE!

I'm actually 95% water, roughly the same as a cucumber.

HUH?

I feed on tiny marine animals that get stuck to the mucus lining of my bell.

SAVE US!

I also have a fringe of stinging tentacles with cells, called nematocysts, that fire mini-harpoons full of venom.

WHAT'S HAPPENING?

And guess what – I eat and poo through the same hole. Imagine that!

IN/OUT

On second thoughts, don't.

NOT COOL

Moon jellies can give humans a mild sting with their tentacles, but some sea jellies are jolly dangerous.

SEA WASP
This box jelly has tentacles up to 2 m long. One jelly has enough venom to kill 60 humans.

LION'S MANE JELLY
This is the largest known sea jelly with a bell over 2 m wide and tentacles over 37 m long. It can even sting after death.

EEK!

IRUKANDJI JELLY
Just 1 cm wide, but with metre-long tentacles, the Irukandji's sting is said to be 100 times worse than a cobra bite.

SEA ANEMONE

Greetings! I'm a sea anemone. You've caught me at a busy time – today's moving day.

And by moving ...

... I really mean ...

... Moving!

And here's the reason why: I'm stuck on a hermit crab's shell.

TENTACLES

HI THERE!

FOOT

Not only is she scuttling along the sea bed, she's also moving home into a larger whelk shell.

FOR SALE

Do you mind if I have a bit of privacy while I'm changing? Thank you.

C E N S O R E D

Trouble is, I'm now left behind.

OOPS

I'm good for her because my tentacles have stinging cells that keep predators away.

They're the same harpoon-like cells that sea jellies* have.

EEK

And she's good for me because she's a messy eater, and I get all the leftovers from her meals.

HOW DARE YOU?

Oops! I'm sorry.

PLONK!

Hooray, she took me with her. Looks like we really need each other. Now that's a 'moving' story.

AWW

*SEE SEA JELLIES ON PAGE 56

MANY ANEMONES

Sea anemones are simple marine animals. Most live stuck to rocks in seas around the world, often in association with other organisms.

BEADLET ANEMONE

This bright red anemone is common in rock pools across Europe. At low tide it closes up to keep it from drying out. At high tide its tentacles emerge again to feed.

VENUS FLY TRAP ANEMONE

This anemone looks like the plant of the same name. It can also close its tentacles to catch prey.

SNAKELOCKS ANEMONE

Like the monstrous Medusa of Greek legend, this anemone's tentacles look like wriggling snakes.

MAGNIFICENT SEA ANEMONE

This anemone can kill and eat small fish, but one type of fish, the clown fish, actually hides in its tentacles for shelter.

ANGLERFISH

800 m down in the ocean, a sinister shape appears.

Dark down here, isn't it? I'll turn on a light.

BOO

Ha ha! Did that scare you? I hope so.

I'm a female deep-sea anglerfish, and I'm one scary critter.

PRETTY LIGHT

COME CLOSER, THEN, LITTLE SHRIMP.

The things I love to eat can't resist the bright light of my lure, a special glowing organ called an esca.

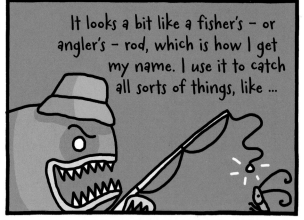

It looks a bit like a fisher's – or angler's – rod, which is how I get my name. I use it to catch all sorts of things, like ...

SHRIMP

SMALL FISH

SEA SNAILS

And my curved fangs mean my prey can never escape.

LET ME OUT

So, if you don't mind, I'm going to turn out the light again and enjoy my meal.

NO, WAIT!

Bye!

Think I look scary? What about my fellow deep-sea fish? There are a lot of us at the bottom of the sea that scientists are just discovering. It's a good job it's dark down here.

REAL EYES

FAKE EYES

BARRELEYE
This fish has a see-through head, so that it can see directly upwards.

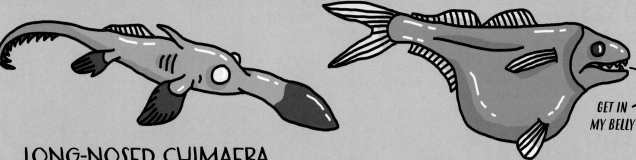

DEEP-SEA DRAGONFISH
The dragonfish has a glowing lure and body patches, which it produces in a chemical process called bioluminescence.

LONG-NOSED CHIMAERA
The chimaera's 'nose', or 'snout', is full of sensory nerve endings, which it uses to find its prey.

GET IN MY BELLY

BLACK SWALLOWER
Fish twice its length can be gobbled up by this monster.

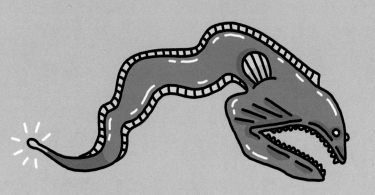

GULPER EEL
This fish has a mouth that, in some specimens, can be as long as its body. The tip of its tail glows to attract prey.

COLOSSAL SQUID

Oh, hello there. I'm a colossal squid, living 1,000 m down in the Antarctic Ocean.

ARM →
← TENTACLE

They don't call me 'colossal' for nothing. I'm at least as long as a London bus, and red, too. Not that colours matter much in the dark.

MY EYES CAN BE 30 CM WIDE OR MORE — ALL THE BETTER TO SEE YOU WITH.

Along with the giant squid, I'm one of the longest and heaviest squid around.

PFFT — I COULD BEAT YOU ANY DAY

I spend a lot of my days hunting for fish that live down here with me in the darkness.

OH HEY, PAL ...

When I raise my arms and tentacles, you know I'm ready to strike.

... JUST OUT FOR A NICE SWIM

I shine light out of my two huge eyes to startle prey.

HUH?

Then I pounce with my hooked arms and spiky, suckered tentacles.

I THOUGHT WE WERE FRIENDS

Despite being colossal, my oesophagus* is only 10 mm wide. I have to do a lot of chewing before I can swallow.

ACTUAL SIZE →

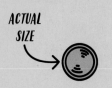

And I also have to avoid being eaten myself by sperm whales.

YUM!

I'M OUTTA HERE. BYE

THE OESOPHAGUS CARRIES FOOD FROM THE THROAT TO THE STOMACH

Colossal squids are 'molluscs' – relatives of snails and slugs. Because we live deep down in cold, dark water, everything humans know about us comes from just a few specimens brought up by fishermen and studied by scientists.

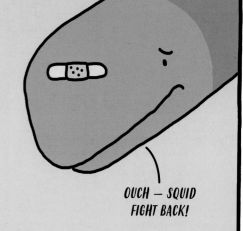

OUCH – SQUID FIGHT BACK!

FIN

SUPER SWIMMER
Colossal squid swim by rippling our fins, but we can also use jet propulsion to power through the water.

We have three hearts, blue blood and a brain the shape of a doughnut!

ARM HOOK

TOOTHED SUCKER →

EYE SEE YOU
Our eyes are believed to be the largest in the whole animal kingdom. They also have a special organ called a photophore for producing light.

SELF DEFENCE
Our tentacles have toothed suckers to help catch prey and fight whales, and our arms have both suckers AND hooks.

EIGHT ARMS

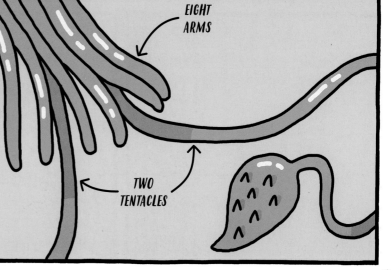

TWO TENTACLES

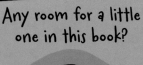

A DAY IN THE LIFE OF A ...

BLUE WHALE

I'm a 28 m-long blue whale, surely you can squeeze me in. I'm not much bigger than three buses in a line, really.

Any room for a little one in this book?

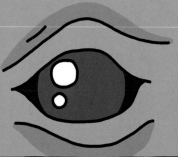

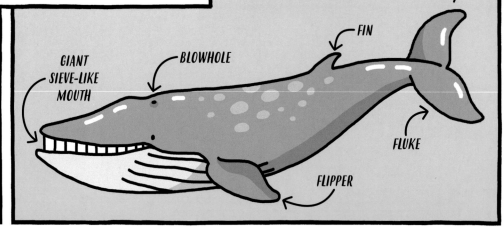

GIANT SIEVE-LIKE MOUTH

BLOWHOLE

FIN

FLUKE

FLIPPER

Compared to some, I'm small. Some of us can grow up to 34 m long.

Us blue whales are the largest animals to EVER have lived on the planet. Apparently, I weigh about the same as 20 *Tyrannosaurus rex*.

Whatever they are?

And yet all I eat are these dinky little snacks called krill.

←8-20 MM LONG→

Although I do eat about 40 million of them a day.

DELISH!

They're tasty critters, but they do make my poo bright orange. It floats around the ocean in giant poo 'clouds'. Oops!

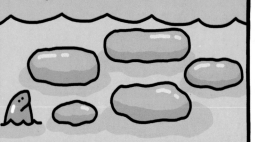

It's a shame for those poor krill, but a whale's gotta eat, even if it does break my heart ...

... Which, by the way, is the size of a small car.

VROOM VROOM

PLATYPUS

No! It's the really super platypus, in its native Australia.

WITH YOU IN A MO!

WEBBED FOOT

Is it a bird?

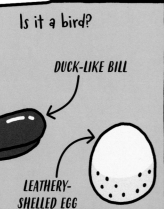

DUCK-LIKE BILL

LEATHERY-SHELLED EGG

Is it an otter? Or a beaver?

BROWN FUR

BIG TAIL

Welcome to my riverside home ... Sorry about that, I was out hunting.

I'm a semi-aquatic mammal, so I spend a lot of time hunting for food on the riverbed.

EEK

My bill can detect the electricity in the muscles of my prey.

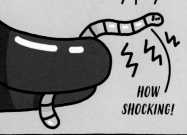

HOW SHOCKING!

Speaking of my bill, I know that it looks a bit odd.

HELLO, DUCKFACE

LOOK IN THE MIRROR, PAL

But I'm an odd creature. For instance, I'm also venomous, which is unusual for a mammal.

STAY AWAY!

Male platypuses have poisonous foot spurs. It can be very painful if you get pricked.

FOOT SPUR

Strangest of all is the fact that females lay eggs. Most mammals give birth to live young.

I'M SPECIAL!

In fact, platypuses seemed so strange that scientists originally thought they were a hoax.

IT CAN'T BE REAL!

But we're not a hoax — we ARE real, so there.

I BELIEVE YOU

PORCUPINE

Hi. I'm a porcupine, living life up a tree in Canada.

My name means 'spiny pig', or 'quill pig'.

SPLASH!

But I'm no pig, I'm a rodent. I'm definitely spiny, though, and I have lots of quills. In fact, I have about 30,000 of them, which can be raised up tall, or lie flat across my body.

UP ...

... AND DOWN

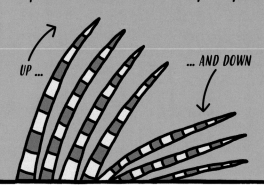

Some porcupines have quills that are up to 50 cm long.

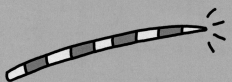

They have sharp tips and are made from 'keratin'.

I use them for protection against predators, such as wolves and pumas, either by running backwards into them or striking them with my tail.

REVERSE CHARGE PUMA DEFENCE!

EEK!

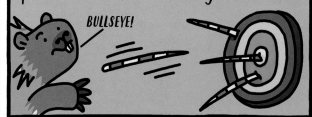

They can detach and get stuck in other animals, and they're really hard to get out.

Humans used to think porcupines could shoot our spines, but sadly that's not possible. Shame, I would be great at darts.

BULLSEYE!

But there is one quite cool thing about us ...

... Our spines are coated with a natural antibiotic*. We're the only known mammals to have that.

CALL ME 'DOCTOR'

This is in case we fall from a tree and prick our own skins, which could lead to an infection.

OUCH

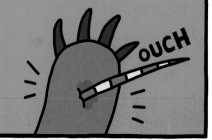

But how likely is that?

BLARGHHH!

*ANTIBIOTICS ARE A TYPE OF MEDICINE THAT DESTROYS BACTERIA

PANGOLIN

Check out my claws! Aren't they great? I'm a pangolin, living in Western Africa.

And just look at my scales! I'm the only mammal to be totally covered in them.

There are just eight species of pangolin like me, four in Africa, four in Asia.

DID YOU KNOW, I CAN STAND ON TWO LEGS?

1 M LONG

When something scares me ...

WHAT WAS THAT?

... I roll up into a ball.

In fact, that's where I get my name. In the Malay language, pangolin means 'rolling over'.

IS IT SAFE TO COME OUT YET?

I might look like a warrior, with my tough armour, but I'm actually timid and toothless. You should see my tongue, though, that's as long as my body.

DO I HAVE TO SEE IT?

Only ants and termites need to be scared of me. I can eat 40,000 of them a night, along with the occasional stone, which helps grind them up in my belly.

THIS IS THE END!

My scales are made of 'keratin', the same as your fingernails and rhinos' horns.

Sadly, some humans illegally kill pangolins like me in huge numbers. They claim our scales can be used in medicines.

I KNOW HOW YOU FEEL, PAL

But the truth is, we can't cure anything at all.

Now, we're critically endangered, so please stop, or there'll be none of us left.

SAVE THE PANGOLIN!

The secret diary of a
BACTRIAN CAMEL

This extract comes from the diary of Ethel, a camel living in Ulaanbaatar, Mongolia, Asia.

ETHEL

MONDAY

What a way to start the week. I'm getting a bit fed up. Yet again I've overheard a human claim that camels keep water in their humps. NO WE DON'T. Our humps are huge lumps of fat, I'll have you know. Burning that fat produces water that our bodies use to survive droughts in the desert.

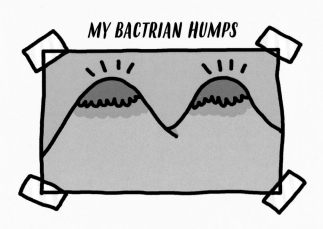
MY BACTRIAN HUMPS

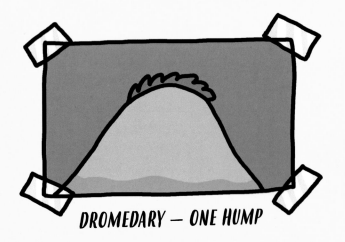
DROMEDARY — ONE HUMP

TUESDAY

Things just got worse. Another human called me a 'dromedary'. Insulted again! I'm a BACTRIAN camel with two humps. Dromedary camels just have one hump — poor things.

Flutter!

MY BEAUTIFUL LASHES

WEDNESDAY

Today I learned that only 6% of camels are bactrians. The other 94% are dromedaries. Ha! I always thought I was quite special (and also very pretty, with my super-long eyelashes that keep sand out of my eyes).

THURSDAY

Went for a drink at the local water hole – well, it has been ten days since I needed to drink. Some wild bactrian camels from the Gobi Desert were there, too. They are the last truly wild camels left on Earth (there are just 1,400 of them) and the only mammals that can drink saltwater to survive. Yuck! Rather them than me.

THE WATER HOLE

WATCH OUT FOR MY FEROCIOUS SPIT

FRIDAY

Overheard another human say my humps contain water. Grrr! It's fat! Frankly, it's enough to make me spit at them – so I did! That's what us camels do when we're really cross.

Ptoo!

SLOTH

Hi, I am the world's slowest mammal. My top speed is around 4 m a minute.

NEARLY AS SLOW AS ME!

I hang out in trees in South and Central America.

And when I say HANG, I mean HANG!

WOAH!

I spend the night upside down eating leaves ... VERY SLOWLY.

WHO NEEDS FAST FOOD?

I then spend the day upside down digesting them.

FULL, BIG TUM

PHEW!

SLOTHS DON'T FART!

A single leaf can take me a month to digest.

THERE'S NO HURRY!

Then once a week I do something different. I climb to the bottom of a tree and ...

... Do a HUGE POO! It's equal to one-third of my body weight.

3 KG POO

This is like you doing a poo the size of a small dog.

HELLO THERE!

I never get lonely because my fur is full of ticks, fleas, mites, moths, fungi and algae.

So, I'll be off now.

BYE

One hour later ...

HURRY UP!

GNU

We are ONE type of antelope with TWO names and THREE important features.

1. HORSE-LIKE TAIL AND MANE
2. BUFFALO-LIKE HORNS
3. A LONG FACE

How do you do? I'm a gnu. (It's pronounced 'noo.') Welcome to our mass migration.

GNUS ON TOUR

I thought we were wildebeest?

Also correct!

Over a million gnus trek across Tanzania and Kenya every year in search of fresh grass to eat. Our herd includes many other four-legged pals that come along for the ride.

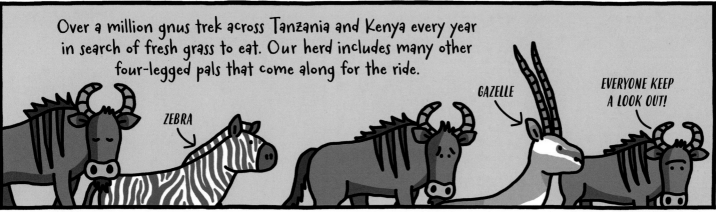

ZEBRA

GAZELLE

EVERYONE KEEP A LOOK OUT!

Sadly, some of our four-legged enemies tag along, too.

YUM

Crossing rivers can be a pain ...

WATCH OUT FOR CROCS, DREW

DREW?

Even baby gnus migrate. They are able to walk within a few minutes of being born.

WAIT FOR ME, MUM

And wherever we go, we always leave behind LOTS of poo ...

POO OUT

GRASS IN

... much to the delight of other creatures.

WE'RE POO MILLIONAIRES!

71

A DAY IN THE LIFE OF A ...

KOALA

Hello there, I'm a rather unusual Australian koala.

What's so unusual about me?

I'm AWAKE!

Being this cute is exhausting.

SOFT, FLUFFY EARS

BIG BUTTON NOSE

ADORABLE EXPRESSION

Actually, the reason I sleep a lot is because my favourite food, eucalyptus leaves, aren't very nutritious. So, I need to sleep to conserve energy.

I spend 18 to 22 hours a day snoozing up in the trees.

ZZZ

Eucalyptus leaves are poisonous, too.

THEN WHY DO I EAT THEM?

I have a special digestive organ called a caecum, which helps me get rid of all those bad toxins.

SMUG

And I produce poos that smell like cough drops, even when I'm asleep.

UP TO 360 A DAY!

And before you ask, no, I'm NOT a bear, I'm a marsupial.

AWW

Marsupials are mammals that raise their babies in special pouches. You certainly wouldn't see a bear doing that, so anyone calling me a 'bear' is very much mistaken.

THIS IS COSY

Not to worry – time for another nap.

There are over 300 living species of marsupial in Australia and the Americas, but koalas are the cutest, right?

GRRR

OPOSSUM
This jumpy critter poos itself, plays dead and goes into a coma when attacked.

NINGBING
One of the smallest known marsupials. It looks like a mouse with a fat tail.

TASMANIAN DEVIL
This is the world's largest meat-eating marsupial. Its jaw is so strong it can bite through metal.

WOMBAT
At 1 m in length it's the world's largest burrowing animal, and the only one to do cube-shaped poos.

RED KANGAROO
The world's largest herbivorous – plant-eating – marsupial. It stands up to 2 m tall and can jump 9 m.

SKUNK

I'm a striped skunk. You can find me in southern Canada, the USA and northern Mexico.

But I'd rather you didn't find me. In fact, if you don't turn this page I'll assume you're a threat, and puff up my tail as a first line of defence.

And stamp my feet and growl.

SCARE!
GROWL!
HISS!
SNARL!

Hmm, that doesn't seem to have worked.

Normally, my V-shaped black-and-white stripe is enough to warn others away.

TAKE THE HINT

But you're still here, so I'm going to have to try something else.

Did you know, I have special scent glands, just by my bum?

SCENT GLANDS

Why not take a closer look? Don't be shy ...

SPRAY!

Gotcha! I can fire my scent up to 5 m, you can smell it from far away and it's very hard to wash off.

MWA HA HA HA

Sorry, I tried to warn you. I'm off now to eat some insects; there's a terrible whiff around here.

BYE!

A DAY IN THE LIFE OF A ... # PANDA

Ni hao!* I'm a female giant panda from China.

CHOMP!

Excuse me for talking with my mouth full.

NOM NOM

The thing is, I eat A LOT. I can spend up to 14 hours each day munching and crunching.

The menu hardly changes, however, and it's not even that nutritious.

MENU
BAMBOO SHOOTS
BAMBOO SHOOTS
BAMBOO SHOOTS
BAMBOO SHOOTS

BAMBOO SHOOTS
BAMBOO SHOOTS
BAMBOO SHOOTS
AMBOO SHOOTS
MBOO SHOOTS
BAMBOO SHOOTS

Bamboo shoots get VERY boring.

BLURGH

Between meals I like nothing more than a nap.

Then, I'm ready to eat again. I have a special, enlarged wrist bone that helps me to grip my food. It's known as an extra thumb.

When I'm not eating or sleeping, I poo up to 50 times a day. It's mostly undigested bamboo, so it doesn't smell too much.

Sadly, pandas live lonely lives.

Other than when mothers are looking after their young, we mostly live alone.

Females and males only get together for two or three days a year.

So, I'll see you around, maybe?

BYE

*THAT'S 'HELLO' IN MANDARIN CHINESE

WOODPECKER

Hello! I'm a great spotted woodpecker, found in Europe, North Africa and parts of Asia. I have a joke for you ...

Knock! Knock!
Knock! Knock!
Knock! Knock!
Knock! Knock!
Knock! Knock!

Wh—who's there?

Me – ha ha! I'm always drilling into trees to find insects and other tasty treats.

DRRRR

DRRRR

PROUD!

If drilling was an Olympic sport, I would win gold, silver and bronze.

When I'm 'pecking', my beak endures forces 1,500 times greater than gravity.

And I'll do it over 50 million times in my life. Yet, I don't get hurt.

IMPRESSIVE, EH?

This is because a special bone structure and a spongy type of bone in my head helps to absorb shocks. My skull also fits tightly around my brain for protection.

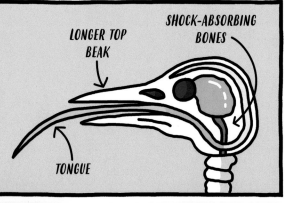

LONGER TOP BEAK

SHOCK-ABSORBING BONES

TONGUE

However, all this drilling really heats up my brain, so I have to stop regularly to cool down.

WATER!!!

Our great skills mean we can make our nests right inside tree trunks.

We also drum to send messages to other woodpeckers.

DRRR
DRRR
DRRR

WHAT'S THAT?

I think I'm getting a headache.

Lightweight!

A DAY IN THE LIFE OF A ... FLAMINGO

Hi, I'm a flamingo from the Caribbean. I have an odd angle on life ...

¡UPSIDE DOWN!

At least when I'm feeding, that is.

LONG, THIN NECK

ANKLE – NOT MY KNEE

LONG, THIN LEGS

I 'filter feed' through my amazing curved bill. Special hairs inside my mouth and my bristly tongue act like a sieve.

The brine shrimp and blue-green algae I eat get caught in the hairs. And they are what turn my feathers pink.

Without them, I'd be more of a grey-white colour.

LAME

I live in a colony that can include thousands of birds.

HEY PALS!

But most of what we do all day is stand around ...

... Often just on one leg.

For years, why we did this was a mystery.

WANT A CLUE?

Now, it's believed that standing on one leg helps us balance when we're dozing.

A-HA

But no one's 100% sure.

BLARGH!

KIWI

Hello there, I'm a kiwi.

I'm a nocturnal* bird native to New Zealand.

My name comes from a Maori word, referring to the shrill call the males can produce.

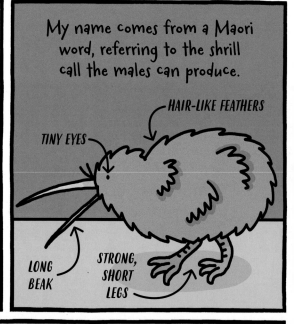

HAIR-LIKE FEATHERS

TINY EYES

LONG BEAK

STRONG, SHORT LEGS

Even though I'm a bird, I can't fly. My tiny pink wings, hidden in my plumage, are totally useless!

I find my food by walking through forests at night, poking my beak into things, looking for grubs and worms.

NOSEY

Kiwis are the only birds with nostrils right at the tip of their bills. It's helpful when I'm sniffing for food.

And we smell in another way, too. We're a bit on the musty side.

SORRY

Luckily, other kiwis love it. We pair up for life.

And although we're only the size of a chicken, our eggs are six times bigger than a hen's.

HEN'S EGG

KIWI'S EGG

ABOUT 50 G

ABOUT 300 G

That's up to 20% of a kiwi's body weight. It must take some laying.

IT DOES!

Now, I must fly ...

Oops! I forgot, I can't. Bye.

*NOCTURNAL MEANS IT ONLY COMES OUT AT NIGHT

GROUNDED BIRDS

Kiwis aren't the only flightless birds. There are about 60 earth-bound species alive today, and others that are sadly extinct.

GENTOO PENGUIN

Who needs flying when you can swim at 36 km/h?

DODO

These creatures lived on the island of Mauritius, but died out 350 years ago due to visiting European sailors who brought previously unknown predators, such as rats and cats, to their island home.

AFRICAN COMMON OSTRICH

At 2–3 m tall, it's the largest living bird. It can run at 70 km/h.

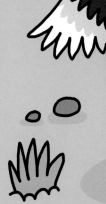

CASSOWARY

This bird has a deadly claw it will use to attack humans if provoked.

The secret diary of a
VAMPIRE BAT

This extract is from the diary of Bella, a common vampire bat from Brazil.

BELLA

MONDAY NIGHT

Or is it Tuesday morning? It's hard to keep track in the middle of the night. I've spent all day hanging upside down in a cave with 100 other bats. You'd think the blood would go to my head. Now that it's really dark, it's time to get some blood in my stomach.

SHHHH! DON'T WAKE IT UP

TUESDAY MORNING

I had a delicious feast from a sleeping horse last night. I found it by the heat coming off its body and the sound of its breathing. I landed nearby, hopped along the ground (a special skill of mine), then jumped up on to its back and stuck my fangs in. It didn't even wake up – must've been dreaming of frolicking through the fields.

WEDNESDAY

I'm still quite full from my last big feed, probably because in just 30 minutes I can drink so much blood it's possible to double my body weight. When I bite something, special proteins in my spit keep the blood flowing nicely.

NOM NOM NOM

THURSDAY

My friend, Velma, came over for a visit. She was hungry, so I did what any good host would do and vomited up some of my stomach contents into her mouth. It's good to share. And, good deeds like that helps keep the 'colony' – our group – together. Would you be that generous with your friends?

FRIDAY

Tonight, I tried a change of menu. We normally go for horses – like I said – cows and pigs, but occasionally we bite sleeping people. Do us a favour and leave your windows open. I promise it won't hurt a bit, and it's good to share, right?

LET ME IN!

KOMODO DRAGON

I'm a Komodo dragon – the world's largest living lizard. I can grow up to 3 m long and weigh up to 90 kg. We're found on just five Indonesian islands.

Do you believe in dragons? You should do – I am one. And I'm pretty scary.

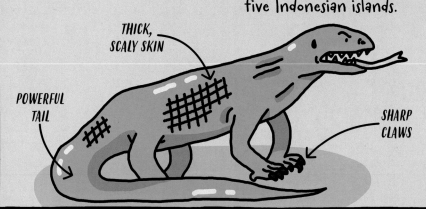

THICK, SCALY SKIN

POWERFUL TAIL

SHARP CLAWS

With my long tongue, I can detect food from far away, whether it's dead or alive.

I CAN TASTE YOU ALREADY

I use venom in my mouth to kill my prey.

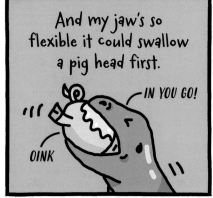

GRRRR

And my jaw's so flexible it could swallow a pig head first.

IN YOU GO!

OINK

I've also been known to dig up human graves for a meal.

BEST BEFORE 2020

And sometimes, Komodos even eat their young.

BAD PARENTING!

Around a big kill, young Komodos roll in poo to stop big ones like me from getting too close and stealing it.

One meal can be up to 80% of my body weight.

THEY SHOULD MAKE BURGERS 80% OF THE SIZE OF ME!

And I vomit up a 'gastric pellet' full of horns, teeth, hair and hooves that I can't digest.

URGH

So you see, I'm pretty scary, even though I can't breathe fire.

COME SAY 'HELLO' ANY TIME!

EARTH AND SCIENCE

Ground-breaking! Earth-shattering! Out of this world! This section is all of these things and more. Plants and planets, snowflakes and satellites, trees and tornadoes – it's a red-hot river of facts about to erupt, just like the volcano that you will also find in this section. There is also a shocking lightning bolt, a snappy Venus flytrap, icky bacteria and a pretty rainbow to brighten up the gloomiest of days.

JAPANESE KNOTWEED

We're stems of a Japanese knotweed, a quickly spreading plant with a bit of a bad reputation.

OH YEAH

People don't like us because we're so strong and powerful.

LIFT!

Our amazing 'rhizomes' — stems that grow horizontally, underground — can travel far, putting down roots and sending up shoots that can break through concrete.

WE'RE FREE

WOO HOO

If you cut one of us down ...

... Another will just pop up somewhere else.

So, we're not exactly the most popular plant going.

YOU'RE A WEED!

People try to kill us, using strong chemical weedkillers ...

... But it's no use.

YOU'LL HAVE TO TRY HARDER THAN THAT, LOSERS!

We're native to Japan, Korea, China and East Asia, where certain types of insects and fungi stop us growing too fast. But once we spread across the world we began causing chaos, cracking tarmac, blocking drains and just being giant pains.

I'M SCARED!

Before you know it, world domination will be ours!

Japanese knotweed is known by many names, including fleece flower, donkey rhubarb and the German sausage plant. But whatever it's called, it's a pesky plant that's almost impossible to get rid of.

UH-OH

DON'T BE FOOLED
The leaves are heart shaped, but no one loves this plant.

SUPER-FAST STEM
In hot weather, knotweed can grow at the rate of 10 cm per day in spring and reach heights of up to 3 m tall, nearly twice the height of the average adult human.

FIREPROOF
Burn it down and the plant just grows back again somewhere else.

UNSTOPPABLE
Here comes another one!

YO!

I AM A MEAN, GREEN GROWING MACHINE!

DANGER UNDERGROUND
Knotweed's root system can grow 7 m wide and 3 m deep, with just a tiny 1 cm-long fragment being enough to produce a whole new plant.

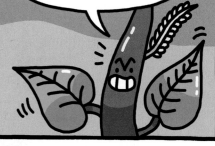

85

VENUS FLYTRAP

Let's make this snappy. Greetings from a swamp in North Carolina, USA.

I'm a carnivorous* plant that eats flies and insects.

PFFT! NO WAY

Whether that silly fly believes me or not, it's true. Just look at me!

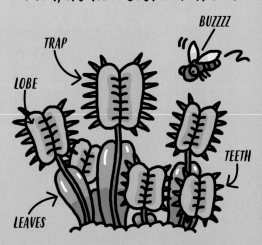

BUZZZZ

TRAP

LOBE

TEETH

LEAVES

Insects love the sweet nectar I produce on my 'traps' – the special leaves at the end of my stem.

MMM, DELICIOUS

NOM NOM

TWANG

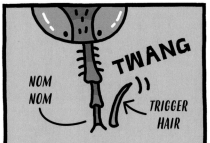

TRIGGER HAIR

Eager to feed, they bump into the tiny 'trigger hairs' on my 'lobes'.

Bump one hair and guess what happens ...

W-W-WHAT?

... Nothing!

PHEW

But touch a second hair within 20 seconds and ...

OOPS

SNAP!

The two sides of my trap snap shut in less than half a second, trapping my soon-to-be-dinner inside.

Having to touch two trigger hairs rather than one means there's less chance of a false alarm.

NOW YOU TELL ME

Once inside, I produce a fluid that digests my meal. It can take days to break it down.

I CAN HEAR THIS YOU KNOW

After just three or four insects, a trap will fall off and die. Luckily, I have more where that came from.

I HAD IT COMING. IT WAS FUN WHILE IT LASTED

*CARNIVOROUS PLANTS OR ANIMALS FEED ON ANIMALS

SUNFLOWER

I grew a root, then a shoot, and then I shot up really fast.

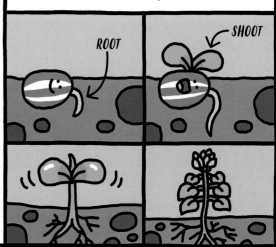

ROOT
SHOOT

I'm a sunflower, growing in a field in Ukraine. Let me tell you how I grew so tall.

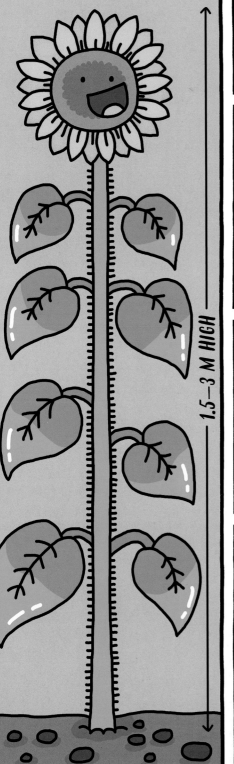

1.5 – 3 M HIGH

I started off life as a tiny, stripy seed.

STRIPES ARE SO TRENDY

YOU LOOK FABULOUS

As my flower bud formed, it followed the Sun east to west during the day to absorb its light. This ability is called heliotropism.

EAST (DAWN)

WEST (SUNSET)

CLEVER

At night, I would turn back east, so I was ready for the dawn. Now I'm fully grown, I don't need to do this any more. But, at the time, it meant that I got maximum energy from the Sun.

While I look like one big flower, I'm actually made up of thousands of tiny ones.

VERY TASTY, TOO!

The flowers that are pollinated* by bees will go on to become sunflower seeds, starting the process all over again.

UNTIL NEXT TIME!

*A PROCESS BY WHICH PLANTS REPRODUCE, OFTEN USING INSECTS

TREE

Oh hello! I'm a ... erm ...

A bristlecone pine.

Oh yes, of course, I forgot.

Well, you are over 3,000 years old.

But you could be older. One bristlecone pine is nearly 5,000! That's older than the Pyramids of Giza, Egypt, built between 2575 and 2465 BCE.

THAT'S OLD!

UH HUH

Wow? And who are you?

A Clark's nutcracker bird. We're pals.

I eat seeds from the pinecones on the end of your bristles. I can also store up to 100 of them under my tongue.

I can then hide the seeds I haven't eaten up to 30 km away, across southwestern USA, where you and I live.

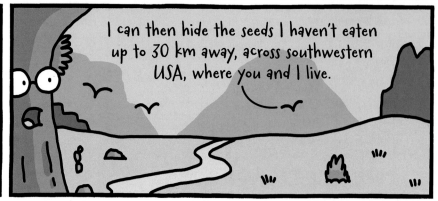

In winter I remember where they all are, and have myself a feast!

SO FULL

And the ones I don't eat grow into new trees.

Thanks, friend!

Wait, who are you again?

Sigh.

All trees are special, no matter how old they are. They capture carbon dioxide and release oxygen, helping to regulate the temperature of our planet. You can tell a lot from the rings inside the tree, like on this cross-section below. Each ring represents the wood added to the tree during a growth period.

PITH
This is the centre of the tree, the very first growth that occured when it was a 'sapling'.

HEARTWOOD
The core of the tree, which yields the hardest timber.

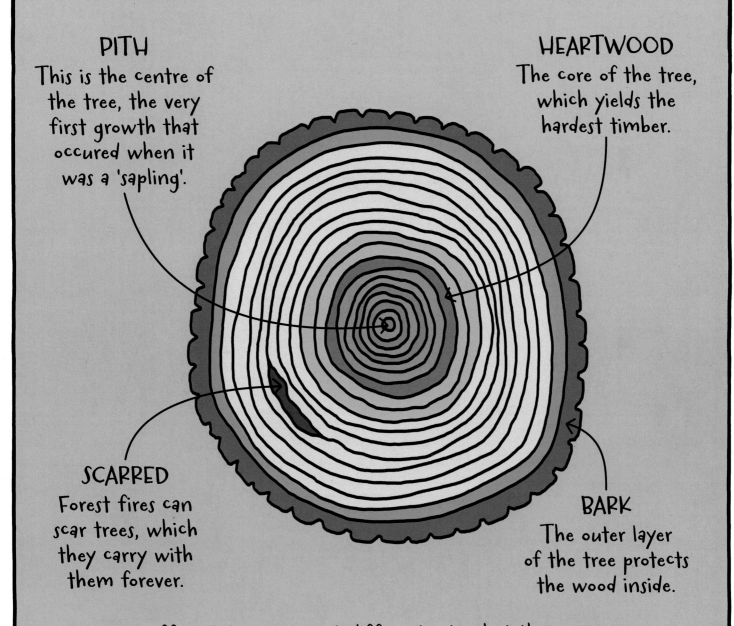

SCARRED
Forest fires can scar trees, which they carry with them forever.

BARK
The outer layer of the tree protects the wood inside.

Different trees grow at different rates, but their rings give clues to how old they are. They also give hints to the climate when they grew. Wider rings indicate times when conditions for growth were better.

BANANA

(In Papua New Guinea)

Hi, I'm a banana!

ME TOO

ME TOO

Look, guys, only one of us can tell this story, OK?

It's confusing enough that we're upside down and green.

THIS IS JUST HOW WE GROW

WHERE AM I?

I'M ALWAYS CONFUSED

IT SURE IS

Bananas are both a fruit and a berry.

WE STEM FROM THIS FLOWER

HELLO, MUM

We grow off these 7 m-tall herbaceous* plants – they're the world's largest.

We get cut down when we're still green and unripe, and shipped across the world.

When we get close to the shops, we get ripened by a gas called ethylene.

NOT ME

We're so full of nutrients, people call us a superfood.

And we're ever-so-slightly radioactive due to an element called potassium inside us.

BUT WE'RE PERFECTLY SAFE TO EAT

And we even come in different colours, like the blue java.

WOW!

SHOCKING!

There's only one thing a banana worries about ... SPOTS.

BLARGH!

90

*HERBACEOUS PLANTS HAVE GREENER STEMS, RATHER THAN WOODY TRUNKS

A DAY IN THE LIFE OF A ...

COCONUT

Are you nuts about coconuts? Then let me tell you a bit about me and my life.

About five or six years ago, a nut like me sprouted in the ground.

This grew into a 25 m-tall tree, with 6 m-long leaves. Tropical areas of Asia, such as the Philippines, India and Indonesia, are perfect places for us to grow.

— MMM, SUNSHINE

After another five or six years, smooth green fruits formed.

Not the hairy brown lumpy things like me.

And they took a year to be fully grown and ripe.

BORRRRINGGG

When ready, the fruits turned brown and began to fall off the tree.

WHEE — THIS IS FUN

Did you know, falling coconuts can be incredibly dangerous? Weighing 1–4 kg, green coconuts kill more people than sharks.

OW

I was inside a fruit like that.

— COSY

Some people drink the water inside us.

Sometimes we end up in food.

But I'm getting hit by balls at a fairground.

NOT FAIR

TOADSTOOL

I'm a baby fly agaric toadstool, living on the floor of a pine forest.

WARTS
VEIL

But I won't be a baby for long. Look, I'm growing already.

What you call a toadstool or mushroom is the 'fruiting body' of a 'fungus' living in the soil. There's a lot more of me down below, known as the mycelium.

Fungi are organisms separate from plants and animals. We get our nutrients from decomposing and absorbing the organic material in which we grow. There are lots of different types of us in the fungi kingdom, big and small:

MUSHROOMS MOULDS MILDEWS SMUTS RUSTS YEASTS

As I grow, my thin, white veil breaks to reveal my red 'cap' below.

WARTS
CAP

When I'm fully grown my cap flattens out. I can be 20–30 cm tall.

YAY! I DID IT!

Under my cap you'll find my gills, where I produce spores.

Spores are small cells that grow to become new fungi. They're released from my gills and carried on the wind.

WOO HOO!

Once they've been created my job is done and I'll gradually rot away.

Oh, by the way, did I mention that I am HIGHLY POISONOUS?

DO NOT EAT ME!!!!

There are over 120,000 known species of fungi. They can be very odd, very tasty or very DEADLY.

DEVIL'S FINGERS FUNGUS

This stinker smells like rotting meat, which attracts flies and insects, which end up spreading its spores.

YUM

GIANT PUFFBALL

This huge mushroom can grow over 50 cm in diameter, and a single specimen can contain as many as 7 trillion spores.

BASKET FUNGUS

This bizarre fungus is native to New Zealand, but can also be found in Australia. Its outer layer is slimy and smelly.

TRUFFLES

These fungi grow completely underground. They are highly prized as a delicious, expensive foodstuff, which is why humans use pigs and dogs to sniff them out.

A DAY IN THE LIFE OF A ...

LICHEN

Hi, I'm a lichen.

Ahem, excuse me?

Sorry, I meant to say 'we're' a lichen.

That's better.

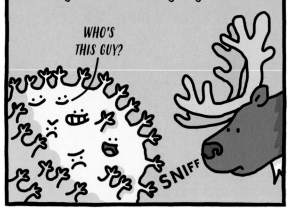

I say 'we' because lichen is a 'symbiotic' organism. That means we're actually several different organisms working together.

WHO'S THIS GUY?

SNIFF

Lichen is part fungi and part algae*. We're a specific type known as reindeer lichen. That's because we're their favourite food.

ARGH, IT'S GETTING CLOSER!

Most lichens grow very slowly – about 1 mm per year. One specimen, called the Arctic 'map' lichen, is over 8,600 years old.

NEARLY AS OLD AS YOUR GRANDAD!

Lichens come in an incredible range of colours and forms, and can be found worldwide and in lots of different habitats.

JEWEL LICHEN   CUP LICHEN   BRITISH SOLDIER   WHITE MOSS   BEARD LICHEN

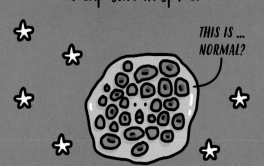

One species, the sunburst lichen, even survived 14 days of exposure in space.

THIS IS ... NORMAL?

So, you see, great things happen when we stick together.

We just got eaten by a reindeer, you fool.

*ALGAE IS A TYPE OF PLANT WITHOUT STEMS OR LEAVES, WHICH GROWS IN WATER OR DAMP PLACES

TUMBLEWEED

Look out! I'm a ...

WOOOOAHH ...

... WAAAAAHHH

... Tumbleweed. I live in the deserts of North America. I'm always on the move.

Although 'live' isn't quite the right word. I'm actually dead.

BOO!

WHOOOOOSH ...

... WAAHHHEYYY

I was once a Russian thistle, and I had roots, leaves, the whole lot.

IT'S TRUE

And, I even grew pretty shoots and flowers.

CUTE, EH?

... SOMEBODY STOP ME

... PLEASE!

But after I made my seeds, I broke away from my roots.

SNAP   YIKES

I now get blown across the desert scattering seeds as I go. I can scatter up to 250,000 seeds over vast distances.

If they land somewhere wet enough, they'll germinate*, and create a new Russian thistle.

NEW LIFE!

OH BOY, HERE I GO AGAIN ...

... GOOOODBYYYYYEEEE ...

*GERMINATING IS WHEN A SEED STARTS TO GROW INTO A PLANT

A DAY IN THE LIFE OF SOME ...

PHYTOPLANKTON

Welcome to the top of the ocean. We're phytoplankton, teeny-tiny organisms that float about on the waves, soaking up the Sun. There are over 5,000 known species.

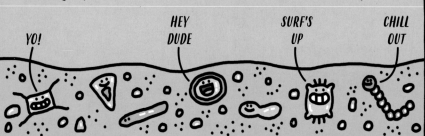

YO!

HEY DUDE

SURF'S UP

CHILL OUT

Some of us are algae, some are bacteria or single-celled organisms. We come in lots of shapes.

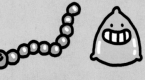

CYANOBACTERIA DIATOMS DINO-FLAGELLATES

GREEN ALGAE COCCOLITHOPHORES

In a way, we're like a marine pick 'n' mix.

MMM, SWEETS

We survive by combining sunlight, carbon dioxide and water to produce sugars. A waste product of this process is oxygen. We actually produce at least half the oxygen you breathe.

CO_2 IN O_2 OUT JUST DOING OUR BIT!

We use the sugars we create to grow and reproduce, replacing the phytoplankton lost to our deadly enemy ...

WHO'S THAT?

... KRILL! The killer crustacean*.

MMM, DINNER!

MILLIONS of krill eat BILLIONS of us, but that's OK, they have an even bigger problem to deal with.

WHAT'S THAT THEN?

WHALES! **CHOMP!** I'M BACK FOR SECONDS

SWIM FOR YOUR LIVES!

*CRUSTACEANS ARE ANIMALS THAT HAVE HARD SHELLS. THEY GENERALLY LIVE IN WATER

BACTERIUM

I'm a type of bacteria – an organism made up of just one cell.

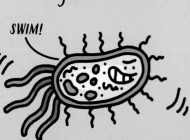

SWIM!

There are many different types of us, but I'm an E. coli.

E. coli live in humans and animals. I'm harmless, but some of my E. coli pals are deadly. And, there are BILLIONS of us.

BEEP BEEP!

GET OUT OF THE WAY!

We're so small, though, that hundreds of us would fit into a millimetre square space.

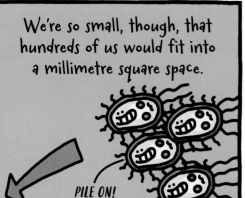

PILE ON!

But despite being small, bacteria species come in lots of different shapes.

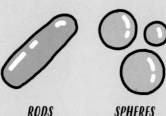

RODS   SPHERES   SPIRALS   CHAINS AND PAIRS

I'm covered in 'pili', which are a bit like hairs. They help me grab on to things. I also have tails called flagellum, which help me move.

PILI

FLAGELLUM

By whipping my tails, I can reach a speed equivalent to a human moving at 160 km/h.

ZOOM   ZIP

But that's not all I can do quickly. I can divide in two to make a copy of myself once every 20 minutes.

PARTY TIME!

MORE THE MERRIER

ALL ALONE

A FRIEND!

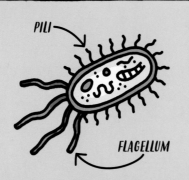

0 MINS   20 MINS   40 MINS   60 MINS

In just a few hours there will be millions of me.

WE'LL TAKE OVER THE WORLD!

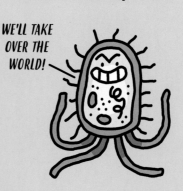

CLOUD

This is a bit high up for you isn't it? I don't normally get people coming up to see me.

There's the odd aeroplane, hot-air balloon, other clouds ...

DON'T FORGET BIRDS!

Grr! Don't fly right through me! Clouds don't grow on trees you know.

OOPS!

In fact, I formed when the sun heated the ground and the ground heated the air above it.

That warm air rose in a process called convection ...

TOASTY

... The air cooled and water vapour in the air condensed to form me, a 'cumulus' cloud.

I'M NEW!

Cumulus clouds occur at heights of around 400–1,900 m, and are a sign of fair weather.

WHAT A DAY

YUM

THIS IS THE LIFE

Cumulonimbus are thunderclouds, which can produce hail, thunder and lightning. They look VERY scary.

TRY FLYING THROUGH ME NOW!

But I can change and grow very quickly ...

STOP IT!

... To become a cumulonimbus – the 'king of clouds'.

EEK

There are many different types of cloud. They each form at different heights in the atmosphere, and only a few produce rain, hail or snow.

YO!

CIRRUS

Wispy, high-level clouds of ice crystals. Clouds that resemble these have also been spotted on Mars.

CUMULONIMBUS

An average rain cloud can hold about 400 tonnes of water – up to three times the average weight of a blue whale.

LENTICULAR CLOUDS

Disc-shaped clouds. These are sometimes mistaken for UFOs.

NOTHING TO SEE HERE

NIMBOSTRATUS

Low-lying, dark clouds. These produce rain and snow.

I HOPE YOU HAVE YOUR UMBRELLA

BET YOU DIDN'T EXPECT TO SEE ME UP HERE

The secret diary of a
TORNADO

This extract is from the diary of Mr Twister, a tornado formed over the state of Oklahoma, part of America's so-called 'Tornado Alley'.

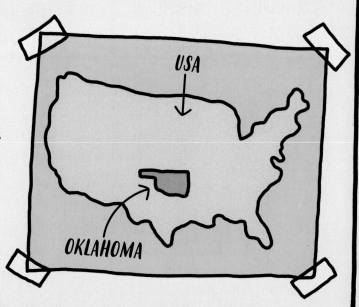

USA

OKLAHOMA

COOL AIR

WARM AIR

JUNE 13th
1:17 pm

I started out life as a thundercloud, or a cumulonimbus* to be exact. I formed when a mass of warm, moist air met cold, dry air above, which quickly developed into a storm.

1:28 pm

In all the commotion, the rising air started moving upwards very quickly. Winds from various directions caused the air to rotate. This began the process of my insides starting to spin.

HERE I GO ...

STRONG WIND

*SEE PAGES 98 AND 99 FOR MORE INFORMATION ON CLOUDS

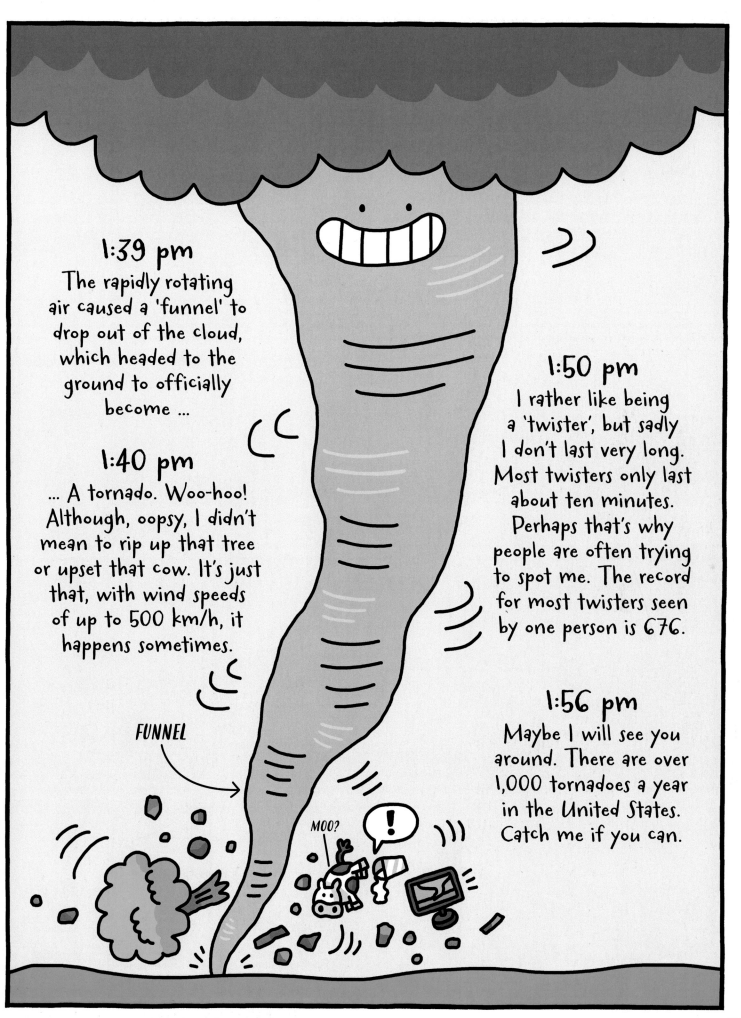

1:39 pm
The rapidly rotating air caused a 'funnel' to drop out of the cloud, which headed to the ground to officially become ...

1:40 pm
... A tornado. Woo-hoo! Although, oopsy, I didn't mean to rip up that tree or upset that cow. It's just that, with wind speeds of up to 500 km/h, it happens sometimes.

FUNNEL

1:50 pm
I rather like being a 'twister', but sadly I don't last very long. Most twisters only last about ten minutes. Perhaps that's why people are often trying to spot me. The record for most twisters seen by one person is 676.

1:56 pm
Maybe I will see you around. There are over 1,000 tornadoes a year in the United States. Catch me if you can.

MOO?

!

ROCK

Welcome to my 'quarry', where lumps of granite like me are dug out of the ground.

I know what you're thinking – I must live an exciting, rock-star life!

Well, it was quite exciting to begin with. I formed over a billion years ago, in the blistering heat and high pressure of a volcano.

WARM IN HERE, EH?

YOU COULD SAY THAT

But since then, I've mostly been watching the years go by.

WHERE DOES THE TIME GO?

I saw 'multicellular life' – tiny organisms with more than one cell – develop billions of years ago ...

WEIRD

... 'Trilobytes', critters with their skeletons on their outsides, about 520 million years ago.

FRIENDS!

400 million years ago, fish came along. Splashy little fellows.

YAWN

About 280 million years ago, the earliest dinosaurs said 'hello'.

YOU DON'T SCARE ME

And, 66 million years ago, they said 'goodbye'.

GULP

There was also that time about 400,000 years ago when woolly mammoths roamed the world.

THEY LOOK WARM

You lot came along 200,000 years ago. And now ...

... Granite like me gets turned into kitchens. What a world!

*AN EON IS AN INDEFINITE AND VERY LONG PERIOD OF TIME

Find out more about my rocky pals, below. Some of them seem to have had much more interesting times than me. Game of Rock, Paper, Scissors, anyone?

IGNEOUS ROCKS

These were formed from molten magma (below ground) or from volcanic lava (above ground).

Basalt is the most common volcanic rock on Earth.

Pumice is blown out of volcanoes. It's light enough to float on water.

Kimberlite is hardened magma that can contain diamonds.

FANCY

SEDIMENTARY ROCKS

These were formed from the build up of other rocks and minerals, or pieces of once-living organisms.

Shale, made from compressed mud, clay and minerals, sometimes contains fossils.

Coal is a rock that burns. It's formed from plants that lived over 250 million years ago.

Limestone is rock that formed from the hard parts of tiny marine life.

METAMORPHIC ROCKS

These are rocks that have been changed by heat or pressure underground.

I HATE RAIN

Slate can be used for roofing.

Lapis lazuli is used for paints and ornaments.

SURE, WALK ON ME, IT'S FINE

Marble is used for statues, floors and walls.

VOLCANO

Hi. I'm Mount Etna in Sicily, Italy, and I'm about to explode.

3,320 M HIGH

KER-BOOM!

Oops, sorry! I have molten rock, known as magma, inside me that I just have to get out. Once out, it's known as lava.

ASH CLOUD

LAVA FLOW

I formed when two rocky plates of the Earth's crust collided.

MOVE!

YOU MOVE!

MANTLE (EXTREMELY HOT, SOLID ROCK)

One plate got pushed under the other, causing some of the mantle to melt. This molten rock then rose up to the surface to become me, a volcano.

I WIN

ETNA

DOWN I GO

MAGMA

I'm over 500,000 years old, but I'm still an 'active' volcano, not like those sleepy 'dormant' volcanoes that have stopped erupting.

DORMANT

ZZZ

Tourists love it when I let off steam – over a million of them visit me each year.

SAY 'KABOOM'

Volcanoes can wreck entire cities. Mount Vesuvius completely destroyed the ancient Italian cities of Pompeii and Herculaneum in 79 CE.

ERM, RUN?

So watch out! Uh-oh, here I go again.

Look out below!

OUCH

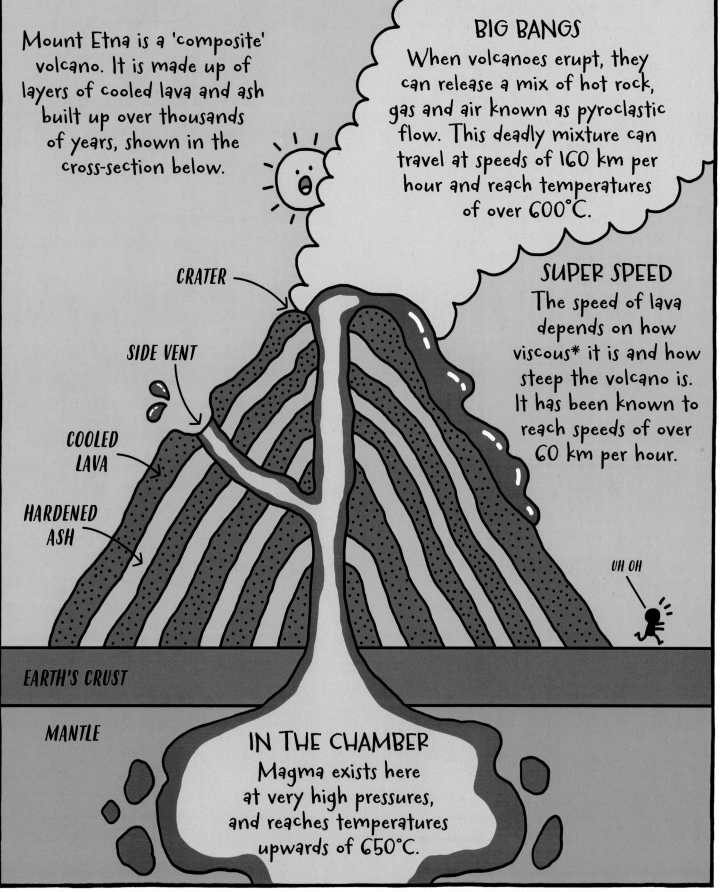

Mount Etna is a 'composite' volcano. It is made up of layers of cooled lava and ash built up over thousands of years, shown in the cross-section below.

BIG BANGS
When volcanoes erupt, they can release a mix of hot rock, gas and air known as pyroclastic flow. This deadly mixture can travel at speeds of 160 km per hour and reach temperatures of over 600°C.

SUPER SPEED
The speed of lava depends on how viscous* it is and how steep the volcano is. It has been known to reach speeds of over 60 km per hour.

CRATER

SIDE VENT

COOLED LAVA

HARDENED ASH

UH OH

EARTH'S CRUST

MANTLE

IN THE CHAMBER
Magma exists here at very high pressures, and reaches temperatures upwards of 650°C.

*VISCOUS LIQUIDS ARE THICK AND STICKY

The secret diary of a LIGHTNING BOLT

This extract is from the diary of Usain, a lightning bolt in a cloud over Venezuela.

USAIN

MONDAY

It all happened so quickly. First came a big angry storm cloud, inside which ice crystals began bumping into water droplets. All this rubbing together created an 'electrical charge'.

BUMP!

BOOP!   OW!

SOMETHING'S NOT RIGHT ...

MORE MONDAY

Electrically charged particles can either be positive or negative, like the opposite ends of a battery. The positively charged particles went to the top of the cloud, while negatively charged ones went lower down. All of this movement built up TROUBLE.

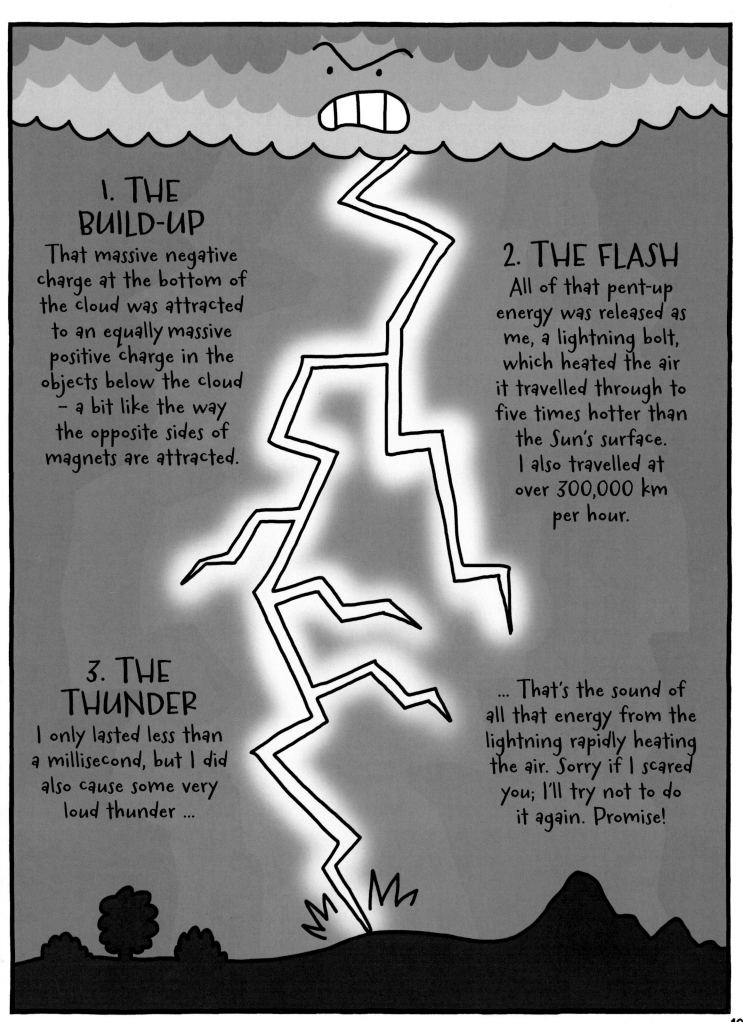

1. THE BUILD-UP

That massive negative charge at the bottom of the cloud was attracted to an equally massive positive charge in the objects below the cloud — a bit like the way the opposite sides of magnets are attracted.

2. THE FLASH

All of that pent-up energy was released as me, a lightning bolt, which heated the air it travelled through to five times hotter than the Sun's surface. I also travelled at over 300,000 km per hour.

3. THE THUNDER

I only lasted less than a millisecond, but I did also cause some very loud thunder ...

... That's the sound of all that energy from the lightning rapidly heating the air. Sorry if I scared you; I'll try not to do it again. Promise!

THE MOON

Who's that? Come closer so I can get a good look at you.

SQUINT

I can't see a thing because of the Sun in my eyes.

SUN

EARTH

Ah, it's you. That Sun is so annoying. Although, it is the reason I'm shining. I don't give off any light of my own, I simply reflect the Sun's.

GLOW

Right now I'm 'full', which means that you can see all of me brightly illuminated. However, sometimes you can only see part of me. That's down to where I am in my orbit around the Earth, known as my 'phases'.

FIRST QUARTER

WAXING GIBBOUS

WAXING CRESCENT

FULL

NEW

WANING GIBBOUS

THIRD QUARTER

WANING CRESCENT

It takes me just over 27 days to orbit Earth. And I always show you the same side of me.

BORING

RUDE

And did you know, I'm also where you get the word 'month' from.

PROUD

The last time you came to visit me was NASA's Apollo 17 mission, way back in 1972.

You left quite a bit of rubbish. Could you come and clear it up?

BAGS OF POO, WEE AND VOMIT

MOON BOOTS

LUNAR BUGGIES

Oh, and bring me some sunglasses, too!

THANKS

AURORA

Ooooh look at all my pretty colours.
I'm an aurora, and I think you'll agree, I'm ...

... BEAUTIFUL.

FLICKER

SPARKLE

DANCE

Even if I do say so myself.

I'm a natural light show made up of lovely colours rippling in the sky.

I'm known as the Northern Lights, or Aurora Borealis, in the Northern Hemisphere.

And the Southern Lights, or Aurora Australis, in the Southern Hemisphere.

According to a Finnish myth, I'm created by a firefox that ran so quickly across the snow, sparks flew up from its tail and into the sky.

I'M SPEEDY

And old Chinese legends said that the lights were dragon's fire, blazing across the sky.

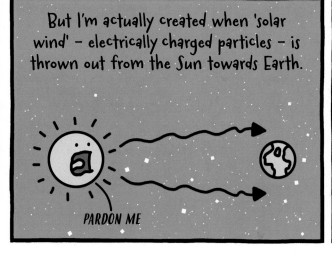

But I'm actually created when 'solar wind' – electrically charged particles – is thrown out from the Sun towards Earth.

PARDON ME

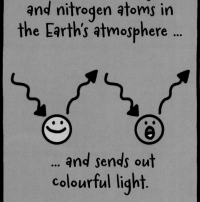

It bashes into oxygen and nitrogen atoms in the Earth's atmosphere ...

... and sends out colourful light.

Some people spend their lives hoping to see me.

And now you have!

CLOCK

Now that I've got your attention, let's talk. You might recognize my face already ...

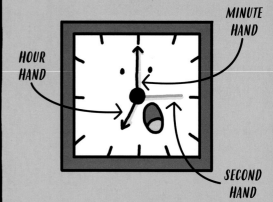

HOUR HAND

MINUTE HAND

SECOND HAND

BEEP BEEP
BEEP BEEP
BEEP BEEP
BEEP BEEP

Oops, did I alarm you? Sorry, but that's just what I do.

I WISH YOU WOULDN'T

... But it's the stuff that's inside me that's exciting.

HAVE A LOOK – DON'T BE SHY!

I'm a very simple 'quartz' clock. Quartz is a type of crystal that has special properties that help me to keep the time.

STEPPING MOTOR

BATTERY

QUARTZ CRYSTAL OSCILLATOR

MICROCHIP

GEARS

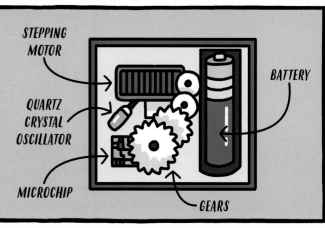

Electricity from a battery passes through the quartz causing it to vibrate precisely 32,786 times per second. I know that because my microchip counts them all up.

BATTERY

QUARTZ

MICROCHIP

GEARS

HANDS

After every 32,786 vibrations, the motor moves the gears that move the second hand.

US GEARS DO THE HARD WORK!

I'm accurate to about half a second a day. Not bad for a very normal clock.

I'M A TIP-TOP TIME TELLER!

Do me a favour and be 10 minutes late tomorrow morning?

NEVER! I'm always on time.

A DAY IN THE LIFE OF A ...

LIGHT BULB

I'm an 'incandescent' light bulb, nice to meet you.

SHINE

Thomas Edison and other inventors created me over 100 years ago.

IDEA!

When you pass electricity through me, my metal filament heats up and energy is given out as light. That's what 'incandescent' means.

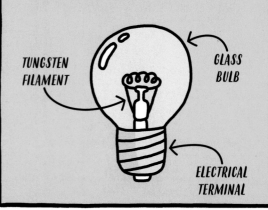

TUNGSTEN FILAMENT

GLASS BULB

ELECTRICAL TERMINAL

You're not a light bulb, you're history.

WHO ARE YOU?

I'm a compact fluorescent lamp (CFL). I last ten times as long as you, and use 60–80% less energy.

NO!

You waste energy as heat – that's why so many countries have banned you.

I'M SORRY

Not so fast, you're not that eco-friendly, either.

HUH?

I'm an LED (light-emitting diode) bulb. I'm the light of the future.

You, CFL, contain poisonous mercury making you hard to recycle.

NO CFLS HERE

I use far less energy and last much longer.

HMPH

NOW WHO'S LAUGHING

So, you're both ancient history!

Did someone say 'ancient history'?

Guys?

111

MARS ROVER

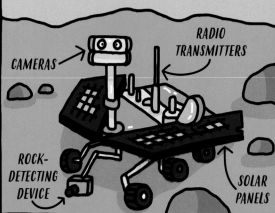

I'm a robot geologist, sent to discover more about the Martian climate, past and present.

CAMERAS

RADIO TRANSMITTERS

ROCK-DETECTING DEVICE

SOLAR PANELS

You came to see me! I'm NASA's Opportunity rover. You can call me Oppy.

I live on Mars, the fourth planet from the Sun.

DOWN HERE!

Well, I was. In 2018, a giant dust storm messed with my solar panels, which meant that I ran out of energy. Now I can't phone home.

UH OH

My mission started in 2004, and was only meant to last 90 'sols' – that's a Martian day, which lasts 24 hours and 39 minutes.

HI PAL

Instead, I kept going for 5,111 sols, and sent back over 200,000 photos.

Including the odd selfie ...

SAY 'CHEESE'

I travelled 45 km in total – a record for a space rover.

1

Now I don't get around much.

But the view is pretty spectacular. This was the last panorama I sent back in 2018. Nice, huh? Come rescue me soon, please.

HOME

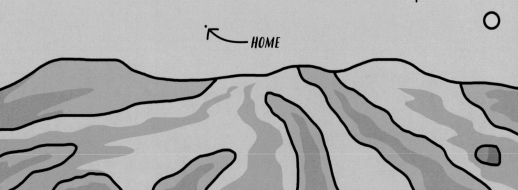

LEFT ON MARS

Luckily, I'm not completely alone on Mars. Along with my twin rover, Spirit, there are many other crashed and abandoned spacecraft marooned here. We're true pioneers.

OOPS

MARS 3
A Russian lander lost on Mars in 1971. It lasted about 20 seconds before ceasing to work.

VIKING 1
This American lander arrived in 1976. It completed 2,245 sols of service – a record for the time.

I'M A STAR

BEAGLE 2
A European probe, assumed to have crashed on Mars on Christmas Day, 2003.

SOJOURNER
This rover landed in 1997. It made a cameo in the hit book and film *The Martian*.

The secret diary of a
SPACE PROBE

This extract is from the diary of Voyager 1, a space probe launched by NASA on 5th September, 1977, and currently the furthest human-made object from Earth.

VOYAGER 1

6th SEPTEMBER, 1977

The day after I was blasted into space by a giant rocket, I looked back to take my first photo of the Earth and the Moon. My mission would take me to the edge of the Solar System and beyond – never to return.

GOOD LUCK, FRIEND

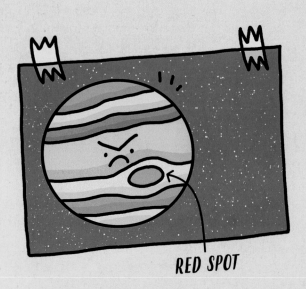

RED SPOT

5th MARCH, 1979

Today I made my closest approach to Jupiter – the first goal of my mission. The weather doesn't look great down there. That red spot is a raging storm with winds that can reach speeds of up to 600 km per hour. I think I'll stay up in space, out of the way.

9th NOVEMBER, 1980

Today I made my closest approach to Saturn, my second mission goal. While there, I spotted three undiscovered moons: Atlas, Prometheus and Pandora. Pity they couldn't name one after me.

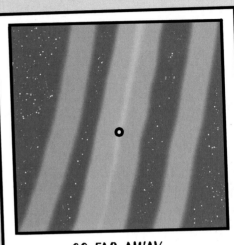

SO FAR AWAY ...

14th FEBRUARY, 1990

Six billion km from home, drifting through space, I take my last ever photo. Earth appears as just a pale blue dot in the vastness of space.

5th SEPTEMBER, 2017

It's the 40th anniversary of my launch. I have no one to celebrate it with, though. I might play my Golden Record to keep my spirits up. It contains lots of sounds of home, including music and greetings from Earth. I carry it just in case I bump into aliens.

PRESENT

Over 22 billion km from home, I am now outside the Solar System in 'interstellar' space. It's great being the most-travelled human-made object in history, but please don't forget me. You can track my progress on NASA's website, if you want to know more.

MISS YOU!

THE SUN

Hello! I'm the Sun, your nearest star.

Although, I'm not THAT near. In fact, I'm 149.6 million km away.

WOW!

That's so far that the light I produce takes about eight minutes to get from me to you.

TAKE YOUR TIME, PAL

I'm at the very centre of the Solar System. There are eight planets orbiting me – the biggest is Jupiter and the smallest is Mercury – as well as moons, comets, icy rocks and gases.

MERCURY VENUS EARTH MARS ASTEROID BELT JUPITER SATURN URANUS NEPTUNE

I'm so big you could fit a million Earths inside me.

STILL ROOM FOR MORE!

And I make up 99% of ALL matter in the Solar System.

HEAVY!

And you can find me here in the Milky Way, a galaxy made up of billions of stars.

Right now, I'm what's known as a 'yellow dwarf' star. But one day I will get bigger and become a 'red giant', gobbling up Mercury, Venus and possibly even Earth.

BIG BIGGER BIGGEST! ERM, WHAT'S HAPPENING?

But don't worry, that's not for another 5 billion years. Until then, I'll probably just put my feet up.

I formed about 4.6 billion years ago, after a giant cloud of gas, called a nebula, drew together. I provide the light and heat that allows life on Earth to thrive. No need to thank me or anything, though – it's cool.

CORE
Here, atoms of hydrogen fuse to become helium in what's known as thermonuclear reactions.

INNER SUN
The energy created in the core moves up through the radiative and convection zones.

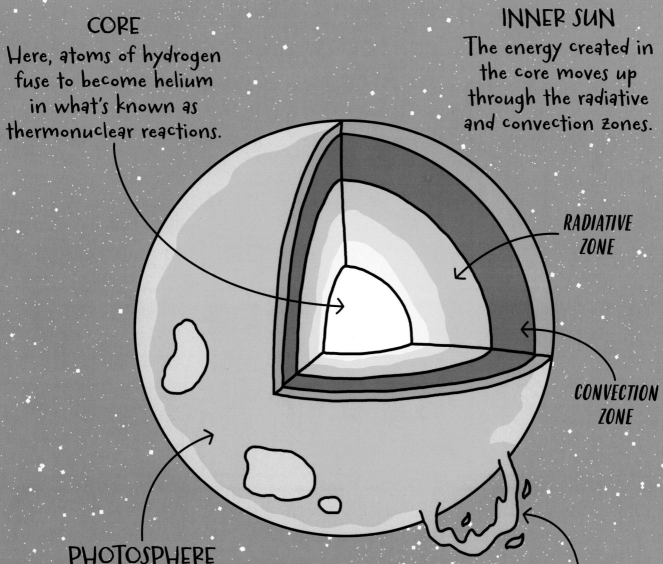

RADIATIVE ZONE

CONVECTION ZONE

PHOTOSPHERE
This is the visible surface of the Sun, which emits the light that reaches Earth. It's a layer about 400 km thick.

SOLAR PROMINENCE
Red, glowing loops of plasma can be ejected from the Sun, flowing along magnetic fields generated by the star's internal movement.

SNOWFLAKE

Deep inside a very cold cloud ...

... It's me! A snowflake. I've just formed.

I know what you're thinking – I'm not the right shape. But all snowflakes start out as hexagons.

THAT'S RIGHT

IT'S TRUE

I form when water vapour freezes round a dust particle floating in the cloud. Or, if it's cold enough, I form directly from the water vapour in the cloud itself.

THIS IS DEFINITELY HAT AND SCARF WEATHER

I grow bigger as more freezing water is added, until I make one of the pretty shapes snowflakes are famous for.

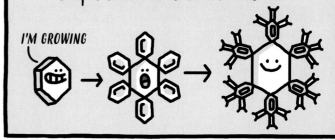

I'M GROWING

There are lots of different snowflake shapes, it just depends on how cold and wet the cloud is as to which ones form.

NEEDLES   THIN PLATES   DENDRITES   COLUMNS

And no two snowflakes are ever the same.

I'M UNIQUE

Eventually, I'm heavy enough to fall through the cloud.

WOO HOO!

And I'm on my way down to the ground below.

THERE'LL NEVER BE ANOTHER ONE LIKE IT ... SOB

I'm going to be in a snowman!

WOO HOO!

A DAY IN THE LIFE OF AN ... ICEBERG

People think it's dull being an iceberg.

This is all anyone sees of me.

120 M

They just don't realize that I have hidden depths. About 90% of me lies under the water.

STILL LOOKS DULL, PAL

I formed when I broke away from a glacier – a huge mass of slow-moving ice.

FREEDOM!

I'm from the Greenland ice sheet, a vast glacier in the Arctic, up here ...

... But us icebergs also form down here in the Antarctic.

Icebergs come in lots of different shapes and sizes:

 **TABULAR: FLAT TOPPED**

 WEDGE: STEEP AND SLOPING

 **DRYDOCK: KNOWN FOR ITS U-SHAPE**

 DOMED: SMOOTH AND ROUND TOPPED

 **PINNACLE: COMES WITH SPIRES**

 **BLOCKY: STEEP VERTICAL SIDES**

Icebergs less than about 5 m wide are known as growlers. I'll become one, eventually, as I begin to melt.

 **ROAR!**

But for now I'm a dull old iceberg. Nothing ever happens to me.

Oh well. Catch you later!

A DAY IN THE LIFE OF A ...

RAINBOW

I'm a rainbow. Can you see me?

I ask because you can only see a rainbow if you're in the right place at the right time.

You need water droplets in front of you and sunlight coming from behind you.

SUNLIGHT

OOOH ISN'T IT LOVELY?

Sunlight is made up of different colours that look white when we see them mixed together. However, when 'white' sunlight hits water droplets, it is 'refracted' – split up – into its many colours. These colours are then reflected off the back of the water droplet to create rainbows.

OOH ... IT TICKLES!

These colours are called a spectrum. We say it has seven colours.

RED
ORANGE
YELLOW
GREEN
BLUE
INDIGO
VIOLET

But there are actually many more colours in between, and they all blend seamlessly together.

They say you can find a pot of gold at the end of me ...

... But that's not true. I don't have an end at all, because I'm just a trick of the light.

SORRY ABOUT THAT

One thing that does end, though, is this book. We hope you enjoyed our days.

THE END!

GLOSSARY

It turns out that there is a lot going on in a single day, as well as lots of new terms to learn. This glossary will give you a brief explanation of some of the most important words in the book, which you can refer to again and again.

Algae
A simple plant that grows on or in water. They include phytoplankton and seaweeds.

Aquatic
Animals or plants that are 'aquatic' live on or in water. 'Semi-aquatic' animals live partly on or in the water and partly on land.

Atom
The smallest particle of a chemical element. It is made up of protons, neutrons and electrons.

Bacterium
A very small member of a much larger group of microorganisms.

Bird
An animal with feathers and wings, such as a kiwi or a seagull. Female birds lay eggs.

Blood
Red liquid that moves round the bodies of humans and other vertebrates. Some creatures, such as spiders and squid, have blue blood.

Blood vessels
These are tubes that transport blood round the body. There are different types, such as veins, arteries and capilliaries.

Bone
Pieces of hard white tissue that come in a variety of shapes and sizes, which make up yours and other animals' skeletons.

Cell
The smallest unit of a living thing. Every animal and plant is made up of millions and millions of cells.

Cephalopod
A group of marine animals with tentacles and suckers. For example, squid, octopi and cuttlefish.

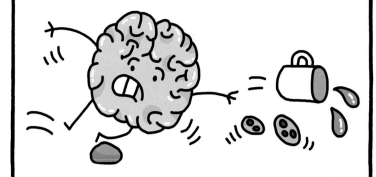

Crustacean

An animal with a hard shell, segmented body and several pairs of legs. For example, crabs, lobsters, krill and shrimp.

Day

Each period of 24 hours, when the Earth turns once on its axis.

Desert

A region of the Earth that is usually very hot, has very little rainfall and supports only sparse vegetation and animals.

Digestion

The process of breaking down foods to be absorbed by your body.

Egg

An oval or round object, normally laid by a female bird, fish, reptile or invertebrate, usually containing a developing embryo.

Electricity

A form of energy resulting from the existence of charged particles. It's used for heating, lighting and powering machines.

Element

A substance, such as oxygen, iron or mercury, that consists of only one type of atom.

Embryo

Unborn offspring of a human or animal that is in the very early process of development.

Enzyme

A substance produced by a living thing that encourages chemical reactions.

Fish

A cold-blooded creature with a tail and fins that lives in water. For instance, anglerfish, cloudfish and sharks.

Flower

Part of a plant that grows at the end of a stem. They are often brightly coloured and attract insects.

Fruit

The part of a plant that has seeds or a stone and flesh.

Fungi

A group of living things that produce spores and feed on organic matter. They include mushrooms, yeasts and moulds.

Fur

The soft, thick hair that grows on certain animals. It is characteristic of mammals.

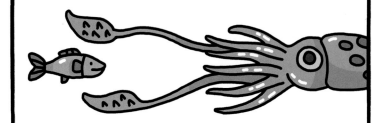

Gas
A substance, such as oxygen or hydrogen, with no fixed shape, unlike liquids and solids.

Glacier
A large mass of ice that moves very slowly, often down mountain valleys or near the North and South poles.

Gland
An organ that produces and releases chemical substances for use in your body.

Hair
Fine strands made of keratin that grow on humans and other animals.

Hormone
A chemical that is made in the body, which oversees the activity of cells, tissues or organs.

Insect
A small animal with six legs and a segmented body made up of three sections: the head, the thorax and the abdomen.

Invertebrate
An animal without a backbone, such as slugs, snails, spiders and insects. They make up the largest group in the animal kingdom.

Keratin
A type of protein that occurs in your skin and hair. It also occurs in rhino horns, fish scales, the beaks of birds and in the skin of most animals.

Light
This is the brightness that allows us to see the world around us. It is a form of 'electromagnetic radiation'.

Liquid
A substance that flows freely, such as water or oil.

Mammal
A warm-blooded animal with a backbone, that has hair and gives birth to live young. For example, humans, horses and dogs.

Marsupial
A mammal that carries its young in a pouch. For example, kangaroos and koalas.

Mechanism
Parts of a machine that work together to perform a particular function.

Mollusc
A type of invertebrate animal with a soft body and sometimes with a hard shell. For example, slugs, snails and squids.

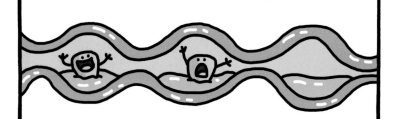

Moon
The Moon is a spherical, rocky body that orbits the Earth. Other planets also have moons, such as Mars. Its moons are called Phobos and Deimos.

Muscle
A band of tissues in animals' bodies that can contract to produce movement.

Nerves
Long, thin fibres that transmit messages from your brain or spinal cord to muscles and organs in your body.

Organ
A part of your body with a specific function. For example, heart, lungs and liver.

Organism
An individual life form, including animals, plants, fungi and bacteria.

Particle
A piece of matter even smaller than an atom, such as an electron or a proton.

Planet
A large, round object in space that orbits its nearby star. For example, Earth, Mars, Venus and Jupiter. Planets are larger than moons or asteroids.

Plant
A living thing with stems, roots and leaves, which usually grows in the earth. For example, shrubs, trees, grasses and mosses.

Poo
The (usually) solid, smelly and not very pleasant waste substance of humans and other animals.

Predator
An animal that kills and eats other animals to survive.

Prey
A creature hunted and killed by predators for food.

Primate
A mammal of the group that includes humans, apes, monkeys and lemurs. In relation to body weight, their brains are the largest of all land-dwelling animals.

Reproduction
The process by which living things, such as animals, plants, bacteria and other organisms, produce one or more individuals, known as offspring.

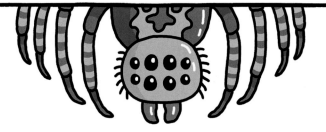

Reptile
Cold-blooded, egg-laying animals, which often have scales. For example, snakes, lizards, crocodiles and turtles.

Roots
The part of a plant or tree that attaches it to the ground, usually underground. A plant will have a collection of roots.

Scales
Small, flat pieces of hardened skin that typically overlap each other, protecting the bodies of fish or reptiles.

Senses
The physical abilities of touch, hearing, smell, sight and taste, which help the body perceive the world around it.

Solar System
The Sun and the objects that orbit around it, such as the eight planets, their moons, smaller 'dwarf' planets, asteroids and comets.

Solid
A substance that retains a firm or stable shape.

Star
A gigantic ball of gas in space that produces light and heat. Our nearest star is known as the Sun.

Tree
A tall plant that has a hard trunk, leaves and branches.

Venom
A poisonous substance created by some animals, such as spiders and snakes. It can be mildly irritating or deadly.

Vertebrate
An animal with a backbone, such as fish, birds and mammals.

Virus
A kind of germ that can cause disease. Viruses replicate themselves within the cells of living organisms.

Weather
Conditions in the atmosphere around us at any particular time. For example, sunny, hot, rainy and windy.

X-ray
A type of radiation that can pass through the body. X-rays are absorbed at different rates by different parts of the body, which can be detected by special machines in order to create an image of your insides.

Bye! Come back soon.

See ya!

Look, I'm still tumbling.

Don't drift away.

Where on Earth are you going?

You can't get rid of us that fast. Come back here.

Nice to 'sea' you. He he!

Hope you had a 'whale' of a time.

I'll miss you.

See me again before I melt.

Swing by soon.

It was 'hairy' nice to meet you.

We'll get back to work now.

I was just getting to know you.

Catch me soon!

I wonder what comes next.

126

ABOUT JESS AND MIKE

What do Mike Barfield and Jess Bradley get up to all day, eh? Find out below!

Mike Barfield is a writer, cartoonist, poet and performer, who lives in a small village in North Yorkshire, England. A typical day in his life consists of sitting at a desk in a very untidy room surrounded by hundreds of books, while he writes and draws things he hopes will make people laugh. He drinks gallons of tea while he does so.

Jess Bradley is an illustrator and comic artist from Torquay, England. As well as writing and drawing for the The Phoenix, she also writes for The Beano and illustrates a variety of children's books. During her day, she enjoys painting in her sketchbooks, watching scary films and letting her son beat her at Mario Kart.